Crash & Learn

A True Story of Surviving
a Plane Crash and Financial Crisis

Andy Clark

First published in June 2020

Ghostwritten by Sean Donovan
www.Seandon.com

ISBN: 9798640887266
Imprint: Independently published

Printed in the United States of America

To my father, Douglas J. Clark (1928-2009). He taught me the value of persistence in setting and achieving goals as well as creatively finding win-win solutions in business. He truly embodied Winston Churchill's famous quote: *"Never, never, never give up."*

Also, to my wife, Molly Jo (Panning) Clark, for always being there for me and always making me smile. She often reminds me of her favorite line by Eric Idle from Monty Python's Life of Brian: *"Always look on the bright side of life."*

To our children: Emma, Camille, Doug and granddaughter Zena; and my work family at All Aboard Properties; thank you all for your love, friendship, hard work, dedication, and support through the years.

To those interested in aviation, the self storage industry, real estate investing and construction, or those of you who are just interested in being more successful in business; I appreciate our common interests and I hope you will gain helpful insight and inspiration from my story.

Most importantly, this book is also dedicated to you, the reader. Stick to the pursuit of your dreams, even in the face of adversity or catastrophe - you never know what life has in store for you.

Contents

Preface

I'm a survivor of a 2009 airplane crash. I was the pilot and my 80-year-old father was the only passenger. He died in the crash and I was lucky to survive.

I spent three weeks in the hospital after the accident, and while laying there with memories of the plane crash replaying over and over in my head like a repeating video every time I shut my eyes, I thought, I should write a book about this since it's so vivid in my mind. Also, when I tell people that I was in a plane crash, they are often astonished and want to hear all the details. I thought I better write down those details before they were forgotten.

Sometimes, when you're going through tough times, a word of encouragement or a success story is the nudge that's needed to make a positive difference in the outcome of your situation. I've read many books and I've benefited tremendously from numerous mentors and positive people whom I have encountered in my life. Now it's my turn to hopefully return the favor. I want the words on the following pages of this book to be the positive difference in *your* life.

Maybe you've suffered the loss of a loved one; or maybe you made a bad business decision and are now dealing with the financial consequences; or maybe you're going through a divorce; or enduring depression; or just trying to find your passion and calling in life.

It's my hope that my story will help you through your challenges or, if you are currently in a good place in your life, simply enhance your appreciation of your current situation. Enjoy the read.

"Our greatest weakness lies in giving up.
The most certain way to succeed is to try just one
more time."
~ Thomas Edison

1
Memorial Day

It was a beautiful, sunny morning on May 25th, 2009 - Memorial Day Monday. It had been raining like a monsoon every day in Daytona Beach, Florida, for the previous two weeks; however, today the sun finally made an appearance, giving my father (who we now call "Grampa Doug") and me the opportunity to continue our weekly tradition of flying one of our three airplanes. It was not only a fun time with my father, but it was a great opportunity to get some airtime on the planes rather than let them sit idle in the hangar and deteriorate. Saturday morning was the norm for us, but this time Memorial Day Monday would have to suffice.

Early mornings usually afforded us the best opportunity to beat the rush hour of Embry-Riddle Aeronautical University student pilot traffic, plus the morning weather is typically more stable as afternoons in Florida often deliver thunderstorms.

Today, we were only planning on taking a local flight of less than 10 miles south to New Smyrna Beach Airport for a quick landing and takeoff, then to Spruce Creek Fly-Inn community for the same before heading back to the Daytona Beach International Airport where we kept our planes at our self storage, office and hangar facility, Commonwealth Aviation.

It's customary to do three takeoffs and landings as a currency check for pilots to stay current on their license. It was a dual-purpose mission to keep ourselves and the planes in good standing and condition.

My son, also named Doug, was eight years old at the time. He was planning to go flying that day with me and his Grandpa but became engrossed in watching SpongeBob SquarePants on TV. He would instead stay home to go to the beach with my wife Molly and his two sisters, Emma, who was then 14, and Camille who was 12. I was going to meet them all at the beach after this quick flight.

At this time in 2009, our All Aboard Self Storage and commercial real estate and development businesses were scrambling to make ends meet. Our local and national economy was heavily depressed by the Great Recession, which started in 2007. We had no idea when it would break. We thought, based on the booming real estate market in Daytona Beach for the previous 60 years, that in about six months, the economy would certainly turn around. In reality, the recession lasted until 2014.

We were struggling to figure out how to pay all our loan payments. The occupancy rates at our

12 self storage facilities had dropped from above 85% down to below 60%. We also owned quite a few developmental properties (raw land) that didn't produce income. We could pay our interest payments, but not all of our principal payments as required by our loan documents. Our cash reserves were running out.

Needless to say, this impacted our disposable income and our budget to take the planes on leisure destination trips; therefore, although flying still fueled my passion, our time in the cockpit had to be self-regulated for necessary purposes only.

At the time, we owned a 1973 Shrike Aero Commander twin-piston (made famous by Bob Hoover who would fly a Shrike Commander among other airplanes in airshows). Bob Hoover also gave the good advice, that in case of complete engine failure, to continue to "fly your aircraft all the way to the scene of the accident." We also owned a 1988 red Waco Classic open cockpit bi-plane and a 1976 Learjet 24D that flew with fighter jet responsiveness, in climb and performance. They were all classic, beautiful planes—similar to the several classic cars my father owned. But, like his classic cars, and like my father himself, these aircraft had age on them. They were all originally purchased by my father, but I felt it was my responsibility to fly and maintain them since my father was not up to the task. But, since they were his "toys," I still deferred the final maintenance decision-making for the planes to him.

Unfortunately, my father was preoccupied with many higher priorities at the time; the top one being his rapidly declining health from chronic liver disease. We were also extremely sidetracked with keeping the business afloat during the recession. In short, we had old planes that were in need of more attention and maintenance than we could afford to give them at the time. The planes were a third priority after my father's health and the survival of our businesses.

Having any preoccupations or outside distractions is not a good thing while flying a plane. Like riding a motorcycle, you want all your attention to be focused on the task at hand.

Old planes come with quirks and their own personalities, so to speak. The Aero Commander had one of its own -- a faulty main fuel gauge. We, however, decided to fly it that day in order to lower the level of fuel in what should have been a half-full fuel tank so that our aircraft mechanic at the Ormond airport could drain the tank to replace the fuel gauge sensor later that week. The mechanic had two 55-gallon drums he could drain the remaining fuel into for storage while he did the work on the plane, so we needed to get the fuel level in the plane down below 100 gallons.

I had filled up the Aero Commander just four local flights earlier with 226 gallons of Avgas. Based on my logbook (which I religiously kept up to date), calculating airtime since our last fill-up, we should have had well over 100 gallons of fuel in the plane. I also calculated our fuel remaining in the Aero Commander to be over 100 gallons of fuel based on our digital Shadin fuel gauge in the plane that was operational.

My Mom (center) and Grampa Doug (far right) with Bob Hoover (second from left) in 1985
Daytona Beach SkyFest Airshow

Andy Clark with our Waco Classic biplane at our hangar complex at Daytona Beach International Airport in 1990s

2
The Crash

I tugged the Aero Commander out of our 100' x 100' hangar and did my pre-flight of the airplane including checking the oil, brake fluids and draining all the fuel sumps. Newer airplanes provide a means to visually inspect the fuel level in the fuel tanks; however, the Aero Commander, being an older plane, had a single fuel filler port on the top of the left wing that didn't allow me to visually see the fuel in the fuel tanks during my pre-flight inspections.

By the time I was done with my preflight checks, my father had arrived. I helped him onto the right seat of the cockpit of the plane, which was a bit of a struggle in his weakened physical state, even though the Aero Commander had a door directly into the pilot's side (left front seat) of the cockpit.

We both knew that he only had a few more months to live. Dr. Peter Grubel, MD, Grampa Doug's gastroenterologist, told us that at 80 years old, Doug was too old for a liver transplant. We also went to Mayo Clinic in Jacksonville and visited a homeopathic doctor in Orlando for different opinions -- but those doctors all had the same negative prognosis. With all this bad news, Doug would easily get grumpy about the pain he was in and the nagging effect the recession was having on our business.

Lois, my Mom, was really worried about Grampa Doug and didn't want to have to put him into the hospital or assisted living facility; it was a decision she dreaded but knew was probably inevitable. The entire family and everyone that knew him concurred that an adventurous and active man like Douglas J. Clark would not fare well in a medical facility.

Flying has always been the ultimate freedom for me and Grampa Doug; soaring in the sky above the problems on the earth. Now, for him, it was also a welcomed break from his weekly doctor visits and medical procedures to drain the fluid in his abdomen. This strenuous procedure not only drained the fluid, but it drained him in every aspect; physically, mentally and emotionally.

We taxied to the active runway and I did an engine runup to check the constant speed props and magnetos of each engine. The tower cleared us for takeoff eastbound on 7-Right, the shorter of the two main east-west parallel runways at the Daytona Beach International Airport. Once we were cleared, I advanced the throttles to full power for takeoff, and we roared down the runway.

As soon as I rotated to climb out after takeoff, I lost one engine, then the other. They didn't die completely, but both engines were surging uncontrollably from full throttle to idle, roaring as erratically as an agitated lion. With its 40' wingspan and increased horsepower engine conversion, our Aero Commander was a very stable and powerful plane under normal conditions, so even as it danced wildly from the surging engines, I was still able to climb straight out to almost 1,000 feet.

I told the control tower I had lost both engines and was going to turn back as soon as possible and land downwind on 25-Right (the long runway which paralleled the runway on which I took off). The tower immediately cleared me to land on 25-Right and I became engrossed in the task of controlling the plane and lining it up for an emergency landing. I made the turn back to the airport and everything looked good. I felt, without a doubt, that I had enough altitude to get the plane back to the runway.

My father calmly said, "Head to the numbers," meaning I should focus on getting the airplane on the ground at the beginning of Runway 25-Right where numbers are painted on the ground to designate the compass heading and name of the runway. This is the most common place on the runway for a pilot to try to land.

I answered in a slightly more anxious, but confident tone, "I got it, I got it."

Those would be the last words we would ever say to each other.

"Life should not be a journey to the grave with the intention of arriving safely in a pretty and well-preserved body, but rather to skid in broadside in a cloud of smoke, thoroughly used up, totally worn out, and loudly proclaiming 'Wow! What a Ride!'"
~ Hunter S. Thompson

News-Journal file

Rescue personnel from Daytona Beach International Airport, Daytona Beach Fire Department and EVAC work the scene of a fatal aircraft crash on the morning of May 25. Businessman Andy Clark stopped by the airport fire station Monday to thank them for their heroic efforts to save his life. Clark's father, Doug Clark was killed in the crash.

3
The Call

It was a beautiful Memorial Day Monday morning and I was getting ready to take the kids to the beach. As I was in the process of packing the cooler, gathering up the sunscreen and towels, and rounding up the kids, my phone rang. I scrambled to find the phone amidst the beach supplies and, when I did, I almost didn't answer it because I didn't recognize the number on the caller ID.

"Hello," I answered on the last ring, slightly annoyed and fully anticipating a salesperson to begin their pitch.

"Mrs. Clark?" the male voice on the other end asked.

"Yes, this is she."

"This is Lt. Michael Hackathorn at Volusia County fire services. Your husband has been in a small plane crash and is being transported by ambulance to Halifax Hospital."

My mind either didn't have time to process what my ears had just heard, or I assumed that "small plane crash" meant a minor fender-bender.

"Okay, thank you," I said, not knowing exactly what else to say. "I'll head that way."

I hung up the phone and called the kids into the kitchen to inform them that we were no longer going to the beach because we had to go to the hospital. "Dad was in a minor accident," I said.

I shifted my focus from packing for the beach to getting myself and the kids ready for a trip to the hospital, presumably to pick up Andy.

I rallied the troops (Emma, Camille and Dougie) and headed for the garage. When we finally piled into the minivan and backed out of the garage, I noticed the low-fuel indicator light on the dash. It's a short drive to the hospital; I'll fill up afterward, I thought to myself. Little did I know how coincidental this situation was.

Upon arriving at Halifax Hospital, we checked in at the triage in the emergency room and were immediately escorted to a private waiting room by a hospital worker. The room was quiet and calm. There was a TV on the wall, but it was off. Multiple Kleenex boxes sat atop the coffee table and end tables, alongside a bible on one of them. We weren't there long before a first responder entered the room.

She somberly sat down across from me and said, "Ma'am, there has been a fatality with a passenger in the plane; however, we haven't been able to identify them yet."

My heart skipped a beat as I immediately realized the severity of the situation. This was certainly no "small plane crash" - at least in the sense that I initially interpreted it to be.

I had no idea who the passenger was. I knew that Andy usually flew with his father, but he also took other people up from time to time as well. That morning I had been so preoccupied with planning for the beach trip with the kids that I could not recall what Andy's plans were in regard to the flight.

My mind raced as I tried to remember who he said he was flying with; ultimately Emma deduced that it must have been Grampa Doug. The sudden news and severity of the situation created a panic within me. Now my thoughts shifted to Andy and his injuries. I wanted to see him and know that he was okay, but the paramedic informed me that he was still in transport to the hospital. This news made my fear swell even more. Why was it taking so long for him to arrive? How had we beat the ambulance to the hospital? Was he still trapped in the plane? Was he conscious? And would he survive?

These thoughts dominated my mind; minutes felt like hours while we waited for Andy to arrive. I knew I had to get the kids out of there and back home, but I didn't want to leave until I could at least see Andy for a moment. It was the longest wait of my life, but the hospital staff kept us updated on the first responders' progress and their anticipated arrival time at the hospital.

I prepared for the worst and prayed for the best as I kept the kids calm while we patiently waited.

It was a huge relief when Andy finally arrived in the ambulance. One hospital worker came into the private waiting room to stay with the kids while another escorted me out into the hallway as Andy was wheeled into the ER on a stretcher. I was so happy to see that he was conscious and talking. His head was bandaged up but, other than that, he actually looked alright.

"I've got to get off of this thing," he was complaining, in reference to the wooden backboard he was strapped to. When he first saw me, he repeated his request, "Molly, have them get me off this thing. It's incredibly uncomfortable." I kissed his hand and assured him that he would be fine.

Obviously, he wasn't in the state of mind to realize that his back was broken in multiple places, and that that was the source of his pain, not the backboard (which was actually saving his life). The paramedics pulled me aside and filled me in on some of his injuries, but my head was spinning at that moment and I didn't fully comprehend what they were saying.

Once I saw Andy and knew that he was in the care of the medical professionals at Halifax Hospital, my attention shifted to getting the kids out of there and taking them back home. I didn't want them exposed to the traumatic experience any longer. So, I scooped them up out of the waiting room, hit the elevator and we were back in the minivan in no time. Again, the familiar chime and warning light on the dashboard reminded me that we needed to get gas--immediately, this time. I pulled into the first gas station we passed and, as I was pumping, I got a call. It was the hospital calling to tell me that they just discovered that Andy had a torn aorta.

The severity of that call didn't sink in. They didn't tell me that it was the exact same injury and condition that killed Princess Diana on August 31st, 1997. My only focus was getting gas and getting the kids home.

"Okay, thanks for letting me know. I'm taking the kids home and I'll be right back," I responded as I hung up the gas nozzle and then the phone.

I called my friend, Lisa Delguercio, on the way home and she came over to our house with her kids, Lea and Olivia, to watch Dougie, Emma and Camille so that I could drop them off and return to the hospital.

4
Aftermath

My internal autopilot took over and I don't even remember the drive back to the hospital. My next memory was seeing Andy's niece, Cara, pulling into the hospital at the same time as me. She was a Volusia County Beach Lifeguard and had just received the news through the grapevine and rushed right over. The parking lot at the hospital was a construction zone and a nightmare because the hospital was in the middle of a major expansion to add the France Tower. Finding parking was a hassle that I couldn't deal with, so Cara took my keys and volunteered to park the car for me.

I returned to the waiting room and waited patiently as they operated on my husband. Cara entered the room, handed me my keys, and gave me a big hug. Shortly thereafter, Craig and his wife Cheryl (Cara's parents) arrived as well. I wish I could remember what was said between us, but I had become fixated on the TV in the waiting room because the news was reporting the crash. I remember becoming frustrated when the news reporter said that an 80-year-old man was flying the plane, and then questioned why someone that old was flying. I paced the room, agitated at the TV and the news reporters every time they showed the clip.

Up to this point, I had kept my emotions relatively even keeled (except for the way the TV made my skin crawl), in spite of the severity and unknowns of the situation. I had not cried when I heard the news of the crash; I didn't even cry when I heard that there was a fatality. My whirlwind trip from home to the hospital, back home, then back to the hospital; plus the three-plus hours in the waiting room had been an ordeal to say the least, but I still kept it together.

Nobody from the hospital was staffing the public waiting room that we were in, and there was a phone on the table that kept ringing. For the most part, we were the only people there, so we answered the phone. Oftentimes, it was someone calling to check on another patient, but we tried to find a member of their family to take the call, just out of courtesy. Meanwhile, I was struggling to contain my own curiosity and worry for Andy.

Enter Dr. Mark White, general surgeon and the "quarterback" of the trauma team. He escorted me and the family back into a private room and proceeded to spill all of his information. His approach and demeanor was cold and lacked emotion. In his defense, I now realize that he must have to deliver news of this nature on a daily basis; a tough job, no doubt.

Dr. White was fascinated with how Andy's forehead was scalped, noting that he could have bled out from just that injury alone. He likened the scalping to putting a broken eggshell back together. He even made a 3D image of Andy's head and how the procedure would have to go. Although fascinating to the doctor and life-threatening in and of itself, the scalping was far from the most severe of Andy's injuries. The doctor went on to explain how the torn aorta was priority number one.

"The aorta is the heart's main artery and the largest blood vessel in the body," he said. "It begins at the top of the left ventricle..." he continued explaining as he sketched a rudimentary diagram of a heart on his notepad. "Sudden impacts, like an automobile accident or, in this case, a plane crash, can cause the internal organs in the body to shift rapidly, tearing connective tissues and blood vessels. Because of this tear, your husband is bleeding internally, making this an urgent and top priority. Once we repair the torn aorta, we will immediately schedule the back surgery with Dr. William Kuhn (neurosurgeon); then the plastic surgeon, Dr. William Palin, is on standby to do facial reconstruction on his crushed eye socket and also reattach the scalp tissue."

The doctor went on to explain that, aside from death and brain damage, paralysis was the number one concern. The doctor explained how his back was broken in multiple places and how some of the vertebrae were crushed. There was a high probability that the spinal cord and nerves had been damaged to the point that Andy would never walk again.

This caused me to immediately begin mentally rehabbing our entire house to retrofit it for wheelchair accessibility. I imagined how our bathroom would look with handicap railings and grab-bars. I pictured our handyman building ramps to the front and back doors. At least our bedroom was on the first floor, I thought.

Fortunately, Andy made it through the aorta surgery that afternoon okay, in spite of the fact that it was the first time the hospital had repaired an aorta by entering through the groin. I didn't understand the complexity of the surgery at the time, but. one could only assume the importance of the procedure and the way that it was done because it was paramount in priority to the back surgery, which would be performed the same night, starting at 7:30pm. Doctors literally had to wait in line for their turn to operate on Andy.

Although I appreciated the support of the family members who had already arrived and were waiting by my side, I just wanted to be alone; to process things on my own. I got the opposite of my wish. As news broke across the community on the TV and by word of mouth, more people started to show up at the hospital; some of them I barely knew. A random friend of another family member showed up with food. I felt guilty for a moment for questioning why that person came; however, my starving stomach appreciated the gesture--until I realized that they brought food for just themselves. Yep, they proceeded to scarf it down in the waiting room right in front of the rest of us.

I needed to go spend some time alone. Plus, I also wanted to check on the kids. My friend Lisa had brought her two daughters, Lia and Olivia, over to our house to bake cookies with our kids and do laundry and some other chores at the house. They were exactly the kind of visitors I needed at the time. But what I got after I left the hospital was a barrage of calls from people who came to visit, only to discover that I wasn't there. Their calls compounded my guilt for not being there, but I knew there was nothing I could do. Andy was in the hands of the medical professionals and all I could do was pray.

5
Coming Back to Life

Over the next week or so, I would coordinate with friends to help me drop off and pick up our three kids at three different schools. I would stay at the hospital all day, waiting on the edge of my seat for news from the doctors. Andy was in a medically induced coma and most news I got was doom and gloom. I would leave the hospital, dejected, to go home long enough to have dinner with the kids, then I would return to the hospital until visiting hours were over. Each day was repetitive and agonizing; involving multiple surgeries, opinions and prognoses.

The intensity of the situation was surreal. Andy had just endured another face surgery. He was still on the ventilator tube and the medical staff wanted to bring him out of the coma and wean him off the vent, so they began to reduce his morphine drip.

It was Saturday, five days after the accident. I remember it well because it was the day of Grampa Doug's funeral. I couldn't wait to leave the funeral, not out of disrespect to Grampa Doug; it was just too much for me to handle. For some strange reason, I had this ominous feeling that, in a way, it almost seemed like it was Andy's funeral as well.

Every family member and attendee wanted to know how Andy was doing and share their sympathy with me. It wasn't that I didn't appreciate their sentiments, rather it was just too much, too soon. Plus, I really had no good news to share; so talking about it was extremely painful. I left the kids with family and left the funeral to go home and change and then head back to the hospital.

For the first time since the accident, I finally got some hope. Andy had come out of the coma and was awake. The medical staff was trying to determine if his brain was functioning properly and if he had suffered any memory loss.

I knew right away, when he looked at me as I walked in the room, that his brain was working. His eyes teared up and I could feel the emotion radiating from deep inside him. He knew it was me. He remembered me! It was a great sign. More good news would follow as Andy tried to talk with the vent tube still in place down his throat. He made a hand gesture and I fetched a pen and paper and gave it to him so he could to try to communicate by writing. After much frustrated effort, he scribbled on the paper, "Airplane?"

His question, although trivial in light of the situation, was a relief to me and the doctors because, considering the nature of his injuries, there was legitimate concern of brain damage and/or loss of memory. The fact that he remembered he was in a plane crash was a positive sign. I told him that they had used a crane and Conrad Yelvington's helicopter trailer to move the wreckage back into our hangar. He nodded his head ever so slightly to acknowledge my answer.

The entire medical team was extremely relieved to learn that he remembered the accident. Suffering the degree of severe head trauma that he did, the doctors had been speculating that he would not remember the accident--or worse, anything.

Now that Andy was awake and cognizant of the situation, the arduous task of informing him of his father's death was upon me. On one hand, I had hoped that I would be able to share this information with him because it would mean that he had recovered and was communicative; on the other hand, I didn't know how he would react to the news. It could be devastating to his progress and recovery. The family had already discussed this matter on multiple occasions, and it was decided that he needed to know.

So, I broke the news to him right then and there. I held his hand and said, "Your father didn't make it."

His reaction was minimal; almost as if he already knew. He would later share with me that he vividly remembered me breaking that news to him. Although he was sad, he confessed that he remembered thinking that, oddly enough, it was somehow a blessing because he was able to pass quickly, and he died doing something he loved to do. It was much better than the alternative; dying in a nursing home.

The next couple of weeks were challenging in many ways. Once he came out of the coma, the doctors outfitted him with a back brace and started to prepare him to become mobile again. It was so hard to watch the staff move Andy from the hospital bed to the chair; it was an excruciatingly painful process. Just turning him over in the bed and moving him in the slightest created immense pain; not to mention bathroom visits. Everything was a monumental and painful task.

It was interesting to watch the dynamics of the hospital staff; their leadership and interactions with each other and Andy. Everyone was a master of their craft.

Dr. Kuhn was the back doctor and he was a pessimistic naysayer. He would come in and prick Andy's toes and always find something that wasn't right. His prognosis was always negative. "He'll never surf or snow ski again," he would say in a grim tone. "In fact, based on what I'm seeing, you need to prepare yourself for the reality that he may never walk again." Although his outlook was despondent, I held onto hope.

The ICU doctor, Dr. Ruland, seemed to know what was best for Andy, and she took ownership and command of it. Her positive spirit motivated Andy and helped him pull through many difficulties. They forged a relationship that still exists today. Andy sees her at Renew Yoga quite often.

The procedures, tests, and waiting for results were painful for me to witness and endure. I specifically remember the removal of the chest tube. I really wish I hadn't been in the room for that. They started pulling this tube from an incision in his chest. It made an awful suction sound as it started coming out. The doctor kept pulling and pulling and it kept coming and coming. I was wondering how long it could possibly be. It was an unbelievably grotesque procedure to see.

Then Dr. Kuhn didn't like the spinal scan. He was worried that, even after the extensive surgery, bone fragments were still present from the shattered vertebrae and would cut the spinal cord. So, I was again prepared to deal with the possibility that Andy could be paralyzed from one wrong move. Although he was progressing and had good cognitive activity, we were far from out of the woods.

Even small things, like swallowing a pill, were difficult because his throat was so sore from the vent tube. When he would get frustrated that he couldn't swallow the pill, he would end up chewing them and washing them down with a little water. He would grimace and the nurse would say that they probably didn't taste very good.

Sitting there helpless at the hospital began to frustrate me and stress me out, so I would leave to go do productive things like cleaning the house, or taking the kids to extracurricular activities, etc. I also needed a break. Emma had just graduated from the 8th Grade at Lourdes Academy the day before Grampa Doug's funeral and now the kids were out of school. I wanted to spend time with them and try to heal our family emotionally.

What really aggravated me was that people would come by to visit and comment that, "I stopped by to see you and Andy, but you weren't there" - as if I was wrong for not being there. Oh, I was there - a lot; and when I wasn't physically there, I was certainly there mentally. I couldn't stop thinking about the situation and what our lives would be like moving forward. I worried about Andy and the quality of his life and how it would impact the future of our family. Of course, there were financial concerns and worries about how the family business would survive after the plane crash and loss of Grampa Doug - particularly in the midst of the worst economic crash of our lifetime.

Andy continued to progress, and the doctors had him transported by ambulance from the ICU at Halifax Hospital to Florida Hospital's beachside facility for rehabilitation. I know he was happy to get out of ICU, and I believe the move helped to accelerate his recovery. He began to ambulate with the support of a back brace, a walker, and lots of helping hands. Every step was painful, but God bless him, he was a trooper. There were even rumors of him being released, but there were also lots of false alarms and high hopes mixed in.

On numerous occasions, I would be at home or running errands in between hospital visits and Andy would call me and ask me to come back over immediately. I would oblige, only to discover that he had called me back over because a thought had crossed his mind, which he had already forgotten. I couldn't get mad--after all, he had a concussion and wasn't thinking clearly; plus, he was still pretty drugged up.

So, when he called me one day to come and get him, I didn't take it seriously that he was actually being released from the hospital at that time; however, it was finally true. Three weeks, numerous surgeries, and countless tests and procedures later; he was ready to leave the hospital. It was nothing short of a miracle. He had beat the odds and survived multiple injuries - any one of which could have killed him. But there he was, leaving under his own power, with a walker.

I must say that his entire personality and view on life had changed during his hospital stay. He pulled a 180 and went from demanding things of everyone and telling me to call board members of the hospital to complain, to being appreciative, polite, kind and a more loving person. His new lease on life made him super sweet and even "mushy." Even though it wasn't necessary, he thanked me profusely for everything I had done for him - and would still have to continue to do.

I feared the uncertainty of the future, but I embraced the opportunity to rise to the occasion for our family.

There are but two ways to live your life. One as though nothing is a miracle. The other is as though everything is a miracle. ~ Albert Einstein

6
The Numbers

"Head for the numbers."

"I got it. I got it."

I dropped the landing gear on short final and the increased drag slowed the gliding plane. I'm not going to make it to the runway, I thought. The grass before the runway -- that's my trajectory. I might have to land in the grass before the runway. No big deal, I'm going to land in the grass. I've done this before at Massey AirPark in Edgewater, Florida (when it used to be a grass landing strip). I've got this.

"Paging Dr. White; Dr. White to ICU-4, please," a female voice echoed from an imperceivable locale.

I shook off the distraction and focused. The engines were surging, lifting and dropping the plane like a rollercoaster ride. I took a deep breath to calm myself and I focused on the runway and its preceding grass.

Beeping sounds echoed in my ears and resonated through my brain. My eyes darted to the gauges. The sounds were unfamiliar and non-native to the Aero Commander.

"Two-twenty-one over one-thirty," a male voice said from somewhere; maybe inside my own head.

"He's going tachy," a female said with urgency, followed by a louder and more rapid beeping.

'Shut up,' I thought as I quickly glanced at the airspeed indicator: 85 knots, perfect. The plane titled and rocked as I tried to steady the yolk and control my descent, the grass rapidly rushing up to meet me.

"Code blue, code blue, ICU-two," an unfamiliar voice echoed again in my head.

"That's not for you," a more familiar, calm, echoless voice reassured.

Bam! You know that feeling you get as you pass the crest of the first hill on the rollercoaster when you start to accelerate rapidly? The feeling that all of your insides are being sucked up from your gut and into your head. Yeah, that one. When you start the rapid descent down the hill--the one you voluntarily chose to ride. It's exhilarating. You packed the family into the car, paid your admission, and waited in line for this.

"Paging Dr. Ruland, Dr. Ruland to ICU-12."

So loud and echoey.

"There's pizza at the nurse's station," a different voice said very matter-of-factly. "Papa John's, I think," the voice said, trailing away.

'I'm not hungry,' I thought.

"That's not for you," the same familiar voice interjected, sans any echo.

It's hot as hell. Ringing in my ears. Sweat on my brow. Pressure on my back. Dizziness. Heat. Bright light, then darkness, then brightness. Beeping, ringing, echoing voices. Lots of echoing voices and weird noises from all around.

"Andy." Finally, a familiar voice again. "Andy, you're going to be alright."

'Grampa Doug?' I thought.

"Yes. I'm going to stick around until you are okay."

I tried to talk but gagged on my own words.

"We've got movement," a voice called out.

So freaking hot.

"Hit that engine with the foam," someone shouted.

A blunt force hit me in the legs, jarring my body, causing my eyes to blink open widely. Two firemen were climbing above me, cutting open the top of the plane. Unable to move, I cut my eyes downward to the source of the abrupt nuisance. The steering yolk was laying in my lap. I looked back up, the sun blinding me as my eyes failed to adjust quickly enough to see in that direction again.

"Get me out of here!" I demanded. I wasn't mad, I was just angry that it was so hot and cramped. Sweat streamed down my face.

"Sir, we're doing our best," one of the voices assured me, adding, "you have a head injury, so it's important that you stay calm."

Still, the heat consumed my thoughts. I managed to free my arm and I wiped my brow with it. It was then that I realized it was blood, not sweat, pouring from my head. I started to grasp the severity of the situation. This was bad. Real bad.

A gloved hand reached out to me.

"Can I hold your hand?" I asked.

"Sure. You're going to be alright. Just stay still. We're going to get you out of here."

The calmness and certainty in the voice was reassuring. His touch was comforting, even through that thick, fabric glove, but the sight of it yielded to darkness.

"Andy, you're not coming with me. Stay the course. Molly and the kids need you. The business needs you."

'Molly,' I thought, my eyes opening wide again as if commanded by the familiar voice.

"Sir, do you have a wife, next of kin, we can call?" a voice asked, as the glove squeezed my hand again. "Can you give us the number?"

'The numbers, head for the numbers,' I thought, my hand squeezing tightly on the yolk as I fought to level the plane and keep the nose up.

Then the yolk squeezed my hand back. "Sir, can you hear me? Who can we call, notify for you?"

In a moment of clarity, I answered, "Molly," and then rattled off her phone number, "386..."

Darkness and heat. Consumed by heat. So uncomfortable. My eyelids as heavy as my body and my body as heavy as... too heavy to move.

"Andy, wake up. You've got a lot of life ahead of you."

Such familiarity in that voice. Such clarity in my ears, in my head.

"Look, you've got a lot of work ahead of you, but you'll manage. So many people counting on you, and you won't let them down."

"Grampa Doug?... Dad?"

I tried to open my eyes but could not command them to do so. I wanted to turn my head or reach out, but my muscles were frozen and unresponsive to my wishes.

"Andrew, I've lived my life; punched my card doing something I love, with someone I love. You focus on you now. I'll be close by as long as you need me."

The sound of that voice was beyond comforting. It was within me.

'Don't leave,' I thought.

A pressure on my hand woke me. The gloved hand squeezed mine tightly. "Sir, we're almost ready to pull you out of here, bear with us."

It's so weird how reassuring holding that fire-resistant gloved hand felt.

"Definite DOA over here, extract yours first," someone commanded.

Pain seared through my back and traveled through my entire body as if I was being electrocuted. My eyes burned, not from the heat, but from the brightness. My pupils contracted, adjusting to the light, and vision came back into focus. Movement. I was being lifted out of the plane through where the windshield once was. The gloved hand was still firmly holding mine. I couldn't move my head--or anything. The heat was unbearable.

A bump and a gush of cool air.

"Where am I?" I stammered, my voice cracking and my vision blurry.

"You're in an ambulance, sir; being transported to Halifax Hospital. You were in a plane crash."

'Air conditioning,' I thought as my body relaxed in the coolness.

I felt more movement; bumps and dizziness -- like when a rollercoaster careens from side to side as it meanders down the winding track.

I wiggled my fingers and touched a hard, wooden surface below me. No wonder my back hurt so bad. They've got me laying on wood? What the heck. "Get me off this thing," I demanded.

The bumpiness smoothed out and another wave of cool air hit me. It felt refreshing and brought sense to my senses. I looked up to see fluorescent lighting and ceiling tiles passing overhead -- and then Molly.

"Molly, have them get me off this thing. It's so uncomfortable," I pleaded. And she smiled. Her lips moved, but I couldn't hear the words coming out of her mouth.

"Seriously, get me off of this thing,"

Clearly, I didn't understand the severity of my injuries. "God, this is uncomfortable." Little did I know just how uncomfortable things would soon get.

I felt pressure on my hand again; this time it wasn't from the thick, fireproof glove, but from the soft, familiar, silky-smooth skin of my wife's hand. Then darkness ensued, followed by complete silence, void of background noise.

"You're going to have to take a hard look at the numbers and make some tough decisions. I may have been a little too aggressive in regard to leveraging and growth. But you can pull it off. You can save the company. I have faith in you."

'What?' I thought. But the voice was familiar and comforting, and I was immediately at ease. I understood fully. 'Numbers. Head for the numbers.'

Bright lights seared through my eyelids and the cacophony returned.

"I've got BP 92 over 61. Pulse 56, up from 52."

More numbers. Who's talking? The echoes reverberated in my head; unfortunately, so did the incessant beeping. Please make it stop. What's next, more sports scores? A pizza delivery? I wish my hearing was as blurry as my vision. The drunken feeling was reminiscent of my college days.

"Andy," said the familiar voice as it interrupted the chaos and quieted the discorded symphony of sounds. "You're going to be fine. I have to go, but you have to stay. I'll be watching you, guiding you. Remember, focus on the numbers."

I tried to call out but choked in the process. A surge of adrenaline woke my eyelids and brought vision to my eyes.

"Well hello, Mr. Clark. Welcome back," the female nurse at the foot of my bed said with a smile.

I tried to speak, but I couldn't; I gagged instead.

"Now, now, don't try to talk. You're still on the vent. You have been in an induced coma for almost a week and you've been through four surgeries."

I cut my eyes down to my nose and tried to scrunch my face muscles and purse my lips to allow me to see farther down my own face. The effort was exhausting, and I opted to close my eyes instead.

"Honey. Andy."

I knew that voice. It was music to my ears. I hesitated to open my eyes for fear the voice would disappear, but my eyes became so lubricated with tears that the pressure forced my eyelids open, allowing them to flow freely down my cheeks.

'Molly,' I thought. She came into view after I blinked to clear the tears. I smiled and she smiled wider.

I tried to speak but couldn't. I wanted to talk to her so badly, but my voice was arrested by an intruder in my throat. So, I just laid there, staring at her as a sense of hope and love overcame me. She handed me a pen and notepad. My hand was heavy and slow to respond to the commands my brain tried to convey to it. There was so much I wanted to write but, after a few minutes and much effort, I managed to scribble "Airplane?" on the paper.

At the time, I didn't understand why there was momentary jubilation over my one-word question. I vaguely remember Molly mentioning something about a crane and the hangar. But what I vividly remember was...

"Andy, your father didn't make it. He died upon impact in the crash."

'I know,' I thought. I've known all along. I was pushed against him in the wreckage of the normally roomy cockpit of the Aero Commander. I knew then, subconsciously, that my father was gone. But I knew now that he was still with me. We were connected.

"No one is actually dead until the ripples they cause in the world die away."
~ Terry Pratchett

Andy with Fuzzball the cat and Pencil the dog, 2015

7
Homecoming

When Andy walked out of the Florida Hospital rehab center, with the help of a walker, in mid-June, just three weeks after the crash, I started believing in miracles right then and there. I quickly learned that miracles existed and came in many forms. I witnessed multiple miracles right before my own eyes.

I recalled my feelings of desperation at Doug's funeral and how I felt that Andy could have died too. But he didn't -- and that was a miracle.

Dr. Kuhn's series of lingering doom and gloom prognoses had prepared me for life married to a paraplegic. But here he is, walking to the minivan; one foot in front of the other. As for never surfing again, who knows--at this rate, he might be on the World Surf League Championship Tour next year!

The biggest miracle was certainly his attitude. Andy did a complete 180 from the time he entered the hospital to his release. He truly is a changed man. Albeit he suffered immense trauma, he went into the hospital agitated, demanding and difficult, but he left softer, more loving, highly appreciative, and patient.

Once he was back home and free from the hospital and rehab center, he was even more relaxed. He was just so appreciative of everything and he became so mushy and lovey toward me, thanking me profusely for every little thing I did.

One of the craziest surprises and miracles was that he suggested we get a family dog. The kids (and I) had been wanting a dog for some time, but Andy had been resistant (he was more of a "cat person") and kept making excuses and putting it off. Shortly after he got home, over a family dinner, he announced, "Let's get a dog!" And that's how Peanut, a long-haired Chihuahua, joined our family.

Molly is right, I did change a lot over the course of three weeks. A near-death experience will do that to you. Plus, the whole medical experience was crazy for me. Prior to the accident, I never liked doctors or medical procedures. The thought of needles was not appealing to me. Now, I'm like here, take my blood. I've become much more comfortable with and appreciative of our medical system. It saved my life.

In retrospect, I learned that life can literally change in an instant -- and it can happen quickly when you least expect it. I also learned a lot about gratitude. When you have to rely on others for everything--and I mean EVERYTHING, it humbles you beyond belief. The situation demanded that I be more open, honest, transparent, vulnerable and communicative. Dire situations like mine don't give you many options. I had to change because I was forced to, but ironically, I liked the new me better. My body was physically mangled, but, surprisingly, mentally and emotionally I was in a better state. I was so grateful to be alive. I learned to appreciate the small things, like caring for yourself; going to the bathroom by yourself; getting dressed, etc... I also became more sensitive. I was watching Little House on the Prairie and Seventh Heaven at home during my recovery and found myself easily tearing up. I couldn't imagine how devastating it would have been to the family if I had died. Emotions seemed to run wild in my mind, but in a positive way.

I was so glad to get home, and I was so fortunate to have a loving wife to support me and care for me at home. The kids went out of their way to help me with whatever I needed as well. My roommate in the recovery center had been in a motorcycle accident and crushed his leg. He was in the hospital for over 8 months because he had no one at home to care for him. I was thankful to have family to go home to. Their love and support helped me pull through.

I was a difficult hospital patient at times; pulling out my tubes and removing my sensors in the middle of the night to go to try and walk to the bathroom during my last night in the Intensive Care Unit. They strapped down my wrists after that.

I even demanded to be released and I made Molly call Dr. Pam Carbeiner, Blaine Landsberry and anyone else on the board of directors at Halifax Hospital in hopes that name-dropping them would help me get out sooner. In hindsight, my behavior was ridiculous at times. I blame it on the morphine! These traits were not indicative of my normal character. But, I did seem to get some preferential treatment while I was there at Halifax Hospital -- and the doctors and staff there did save my life!

At Florida Hospital Rehab a sensor was put on my bed to alarm the staff if I tried to get out of bed.

I believe that my attitude about being in the hospital was simply a result of my desire to recover and be released. Although gruff and maybe even a bit rude at times, in retrospect, this attitude probably accelerated my healing and recovery immensely. I was strong-willed and fighting. I had things to do, family to see, and a business to salvage.

Meanwhile, the business was surviving thanks to the hard work of a fantastic team of employees. Their efforts and dedication to the company kept it afloat during my recovery. My second week in the hospital, Mike Polito, our CFO, brought a stack of checks to my room for me to sign. I can't thank the team enough for stepping up and keeping things going while I was down.

It was awesome that I had good medical care, and everyone was pulling for me. My Mom visited me every day. On one visit, she shared with me a dream that she had the previous night, in which Grampa Doug was healthy again. She said he wasn't going to leave this earth until he knew I was okay. I got goosebumps. That was a very comforting thought; to know that he was young and virile and still present with me. To this day, I still think about him that way and feel a great sense of connectivity.

Grampa Doug was highly attuned to his intuition and we often talked about death and the afterlife. He always wanted to have control during his life and, based on his estate planning, he desired to maintain some degree of control after his death as well. Thankfully, he did a great job on his succession planning.

I grappled with the fact that the plane crash was my fault, but I consoled myself with the fact that my father died doing something he loved, with me. No more medical issues, no more pain and suffering, no long drawn out death process. I know he passed quickly because he was ready to go. I believe that if he could have chosen how and when he would die, this is how it would have happened.

On the contrary, my will to live was strong. I was 45-years old and in good health. I had a wife and three amazing children that I needed to live for. I learned in the hospital that the will to live is a very powerful thing and has the ability to accelerate healing and, in some cases, even manifest miracles. It is nothing short of a miracle that I am alive today. Against the odds and multiple doctors' prognoses, I can walk, talk, think and live normally today. I will never forget what I went through and I will always remain appreciative of this second chance at life that I have been blessed with.

My father, on the other hand, was ready to go. And so he did. My will to live kept me fighting to remain alive. And, fortunately, I did.

I'm not sure if I needed closure or if it was subconscious guilt for not being present at his funeral, but I decided to read his obituary. I picked up the newspaper clipping off of the end table. It read:

A Memorial Service for Douglas "Doug" James Clark of Port Orange Fla. will be held Saturday May 30 2009 at 11:00 a.m. at Port Orange Presbyterian Church 4662 S. Clyde Morris Blvd. Port Orange Fla. with his son Rev. Dr. Calvin H. Gittner Pastor officiating. He will be greatly missed by his family who appreciate the outpouring of love and support they have received. An additional tribute will appear in the Friday May 29th News-Journal edition. In lieu of flowers, donations can be made to the Youth Group at Port Orange Presbyterian Church 4662 S Clyde Morris Port Orange FL 32129 and The Children's Advocacy Center at 1011 W ISB Daytona Beach Fl 32114. Arrangements are under the careful direction of Lohman Funeral Home Port Orange.

I sat there for a while, with Peanut on my lap and the newspaper obituary in my hand, thinking about my father and the legacy he left behind. "We all die. The goal isn't to live forever, the goal is to create something that will." This quote by Chuck Palahniuk was very apropos. My father created something bigger than himself. He built houses for many, many families -- almost all of them are still standing today. He built the office building where our company headquarters are located. The mobile home parks he built and managed offered affordable housing options in prime locations to their residents. And the self-storage facilities he pioneered and developed in our community gave people a safe haven to store their cherished possessions.

My concentration was interrupted, and my attention was diverted to the TV across the room which was on for background noise. I had been watching sitcom reruns earlier, but now the news was on. The talking heads were droning on and on with their negative news reports about the economy. One reporter was specifically talking about President Obama's Recovery Act, or rather bailout plan.

No one knew how long this recession was going to last or how much worse it was going to get. Economists were projecting doom and gloom. Banks were going bankrupt. Layoffs and unemployment was at an all-time high.

A reporter said, "A record 3 million households have been hit with foreclosure so far in 2009. And almost another 3 million homeowners have received at least one foreclosure filing during 2009, setting a new record for the number of people falling behind on their mortgage payments."

I searched for the remote, but it was out of my reach. I didn't want to disturb the dog and I didn't want to continue watching the negativity. I knew what I had to do; I had to keep my father's legacy alive. Despite the worst economic downturn since the Great Depression of 1927, I would make it my mission to preserve what Dad had created.

"Molly," I hollered.

"Yes, dear," she answered as she poked her head around the corner into the living room.

"Could you bring me the remote, please?"

"Of course," she replied as she fetched the remote and handed it to me, petting Peanut at the same time with the other hand.

"Thank you so much, honey."

"No problem. Can I get you anything else?"

"Actually, did you say that we got a copy of Dad's funeral on DVD?"

"Yes. Would you like to watch it?"

"I think so."

It could have been the need for more closure, or maybe I was looking for inspiration, or maybe I was guilty that I wasn't present; for some reason, I just wanted to watch the funeral. So, Molly fetched the DVD and popped it into the player.

8
Doug

Grampa Doug was an amazing man and, as I watched the funeral video through teary eyes, I was reminded of many of his character traits as family members shared their eulogies and fond memories of him.

A hard worker and go-getter his entire life, Doug would often say, *"The best retirement plan is to plan to never retire."*

He had vision and the ability to see things before they were completed.

He lived his life the way he wanted. He dressed in his own style. He always did his own thing. If he wanted something, he went for it and got it.

Even toward the end of his life, when things got bad health wise, he was convinced he just needed a juicer for protein shakes and for everyone at Port Orange Presbytarian Church to pray for him. He wanted to fight, and those ideas would normally help, but his body was too far gone to defeat liver disease.

Doug always wanted to share things with others. He loved family gatherings and my Mom's cooking. Every Thanksgiving he wanted to share his wealth and the fruits of his labor with our family.

He was slow to anger, and he rarely cursed. He internalized a lot of things and dealt with them his own way, on his own timeline. He had a knack for getting things done with city officials through creative persistence. He knew how to deal with people and contain his ego and anger.

Doug left high school in 1946 to join the U.S. Navy at age 17. He completed two years of service that the Navy offered at that time. He did his basic training at Great Lakes Training Center and then took a train to San Diego where he helped de-commission warships.

He attended Bradley College in northern Illinois after the Navy through the G.I. bill, but he was yearning to make money using the skills he learned in his drafting classes, so he left school and started building houses in 1949.

He would often build the basement of a new home and live in the basement while he finished the rest of the house.

In early 1952, Doug and his new wife, Phyllis, became tired of the snow in Northern Illinois. They considered moving to Southern California, but Doug thought that the dry, desert area would run out of water due to the huge population that was moving there.

They instead toured Florida and decided Ormond Beach was the perfect place for their future.

In 1953, they built the Argosy motel in Ormond by the Sea, just north of Ormond Beach. They managed the Argosy and lived on the premises. Initially, the property had no air conditioning because they thought the ocean breezes were plenty cool enough for them and other travelers.

Doug was also building houses in Ormond Beach, Holly Hill, and the north peninsula north of Ormond Beach at the time. The plumber he hired for some of these houses was George Baker, and the two became life-long friends. George and his wife, Ginny, went on to own Brookes Custom Cleaners on Main Street in Daytona Beach.

George was a private pilot who was also re-building airplanes in his garage at home. George took Doug flying and showed him how to fly.

Doug became a private pilot in 1955. He joined the Civil Air Patrol and got flight time by flying patrols up and down the Florida coastline. The CAP was founded in 1941 to mobilize the nation's civil airplanes for national defense.

Over the next 50 years, Doug would go on to log over 8,000 hours of flight time. At first, he rented all sorts of small, single-engine Pipers, Cessnas and Beechcraft, but he went on to own some of the following aircraft:

- Globe Swifts (two-place, tail-dragger)
- Aero Commanders (seven-place, twin-piston: Doug loved these aircraft and would own three different Commanders from 1973-2009).
- Canadair T-33 (a 1950's-era subsonic jet trainer restored by and flown in air shows by George Baker)
- P-51 Mustang (the World War II fighter Doug owned was named "Hurry Home Honey." Doug sold this plane as soon as George Baker restored it to have enough money to finish the Commonwealth Aviation hangars in 1988).
- LearJet 24 and 25
- Waco Classic bi-plane
- Grumman Widgeon (six-place twin-engine amphibious aircraft built in 1941)

Doug also formed a life-long friendship during the late 1950's with Conrad Yelvington who delivered sod to Doug's houses. Doug, Conrad and George Baker became the "Three Amigos" who were very active in the local aviation community and in the Quiet Birdman, a secretive club for male aviators founded in 1921. In 1955, Doug and Lois met in the small town of Ormond by the Sea, where they and their spouses owned small motels near each other on the ocean.

Lois and her first husband, Bud Gittner, had moved to the area from Milwaukee, Wisconsin in 1955 and bought the Ormond by the Sea Motel which was one-quarter mile south of Doug and his wife's Argosy Motel. The neighboring couples (along with Charlie Strasser and his wife, the Bakers and the Yelvingtons) would take turns hosting monthly dinner parties in each other's homes.

By the early 1960's, both Lois and Doug's first marriages had ended. In 1962, Doug and Lois married, and this marriage would last 47 years.

Lois had four boys during her first marriage and Doug had two sons during his. I was born in 1964. We had moved to 1225 Thompson Place off Silver Beach at this time.

Doug loved to work and have his hands in every part of the development process, from design, through the construction process, to completion. He drew his own construction plans for the houses he built. The timing was perfect for him as he was able to capitalize on the population boom in Florida after WWII. Like an airplane's ascent, his business really took off right from the start.

"How big should we get?" he would often ask me and Mom. "We're on a rocket ship - hang on for the ride!" he would proclaim.

Doug possessed a dynamic personality that encompassed a weird combination of ego-driven desires that was balanced by his desire to help others. When there was something he wanted, hardly anything could stand in his way.

By 2009, the nation's economy and Doug's health deteriorated at the same time.

He fought hard his entire life; for his family, for the business and, in the end, for his life. The average person would have given up so many times over, but Doug never did. It was like he was always striving for some award for best comeback in the end. He taught us to never stop fighting, no matter how uphill the battle may seem.

The attendance at the funeral and the kind words that were shared were true testaments to a life well lived. When the video was over, I picked up the obituary and read it to myself.

Prominent businessman and builder Douglas Clark died on Memorial Day, May 25, 2009 in an airplane accident at Daytona International Airport. A 57-year resident of the Daytona area, he was well-known in local aviation, business and social circles for decades. A Memorial Service for Doug will be held on Saturday, May 30, 2009 at 11:00 a.m. at Port Orange Presbyterian Church, 4662 S. Clyde Morris Blvd., Port Orange, FL with his son Rev. Dr. Calvin H. Gittner, Pastor, officiating.

He was born in Dekalb, Illinois as the oldest son to James and Florence Clark. He had four younger sisters. Following two years of service in the U.S. Navy and attending Bradley University in Peoria, Illinois, he began building homes in Illinois in 1948. In 1952, Doug moved to Ormond Beach with his first wife, Phyllis and two sons, Gregory and David. He began building homes and an oceanfront motel which he owned/operated. It was also during this period that he developed his love of flying, learning to fly a variety of airplanes.

On May 29, 1962 he married Lois E. Clark. Lois has four sons from her first marriage, Chuck, Craig, Cory and Calvin Gittner. In 1964, a fifth son, D. Andrew Clark, was born.

Doug became active in the Daytona Beach Homebuilder's Association and served as Vice President of the organization in 1964. In 1968, Doug served on the first Planning Commission for the City of Port Orange. In 1965, Doug founded MPC Builders with business partners. MPC Builders developed mobile home parks in Port Orange, Florida, then a town of just 3,000 people. The three partners built several award-winning mobile home communities for thousands of residents. They also built Rose Bay Campground and Commonwealth Plaza, a retail shopping plaza. In 1978, Doug and Robert Powell built Maplewood Self Storage. In 1983, this became the foundation for All Aboard Storage, now with dozens of locations.

Throughout these years, Doug remained active in flying, often taking his large family on summer vacations to destinations such as the Bahamas and Illinois in small airplanes. He was also active in the local Quiet Birdman club, the Valiant Air Command and the Experimental Aircraft Association. Over the years, he owned several "war birds" (military aircraft); a P51 Mustang and a T-33 (Korean war-era jet trainer), and many types of passenger planes. He also kept a strong interest in his first trade, carpentry.

In 1968 he and Lois purchased a home built in 1913 on the river in Port Orange. Doug and his family spent many years remodeling and refurbishing the pioneer home, in which the family still lives. In later years, Doug continued his interest in building and remodeling, adding historic structures to a growing compound around his home, including a 110-year-old wedding chapel, a reception hall, and 1940s-era train car, cottages and fishponds. This property, along with the Clark Office Building, show his attention to detail, creative zeal, artistic touch and affection for beautiful architecture.

Doug and Lois were also avid travelers, enjoying trips such as around-the-world adventures to flying in their own planes for shorter weekend getaways. They were active members in the Halifax River Yacht Club and deeply appreciate the many friendships they have made there.

A self-educated man, Doug will always be remembered for his intellect, his calm and thoughtful personality and his witty charm. He had a love of music and art, collected both old and new cars and was generous and kind with his grandchildren. His long legacy of success will live on as will his large and loving family who will always feel his presence and benefit from his wise guidance. He is survived by the love of his life, Lois; his sons and daughters-in-law; 19 grandchildren; and four great-grandchildren.

Arrangements are under the careful direction of Lohman Funeral Home Port Orange. Condolences can be made to the family at LohmanFuneralHomes.com. In lieu of flowers the Clark family has asked for donations to be made to the following charitable organizations: The Children's Advocacy Center, 1011 W. International Speedway Blvd., Daytona Beach, FL 32114 or Port Orange Presbyterian Church Youth Group, 4662 Clyde Morris Blvd., Port Orange, FL 32129.

~

I dried my eyes and smiled with pride. I found solace in the fact that he no longer had to worry about his declining health. At least that burden had been lifted. There is also a sense of peace in my mind knowing that he died doing something he loved, with me. He is now free from his body and free to fly to new heavenly heights. Rest in peace, Grampa Doug, you will be missed and always loved.

Andy's maternal grandmother
Elfrieda (Berner) Eharoshe (1885-
1977). Photo was taken circa 1912.
She married George Eharoshe in
1917

Andy's maternal grandfather
George Oscar Eharoshe in 1910.
He was born in Yugoslavia (Eastern
Europe) in 1890, immigrated to the
USA in 1905, died 1968

Andy's mom: Lois Elaine Eharoshe
circa 1948

Lois, Mike, Florence, Mary and Parents

Lois & Father 1929

Andy's great grandparents
Mortimer Delano Clapper &
Minnie Jane (Newman)
Clapper married 1901

Andy's paternal grandmother
Florence Clark circa 1920

Andy's paternal grandparents
Florence E. (Clapper) Clark (1902-1996) and James Henry Clark (1905-1976) circa 1950. They were married in 1927

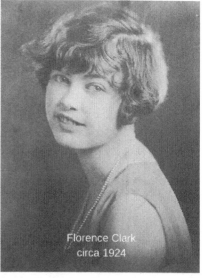

Florence Clark
circa 1924

Doug - Sterling, Illinois
circa 1935

Doug – Freeport, Illinois
circa 1940

Doug – Freeport, Illinois
circa 1947

US Navy 1946-48s

Doug's first visit to Daytona Beach 1951

Building First House, Freeport Illinois 1949

Doug at work at the Argosy Motel
circa 1954

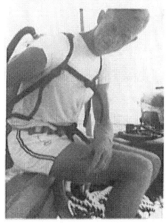

Mexico 1961

Certificate of Marriage

THIS CERTIFIES THAT

Douglas James Clark OF Ormond Beach, Fla

AND Lois Elaine Gittner OF Ormond Beach, Fla

WERE UNITED IN MARRIAGE ACCORDING TO THE TEACHING OF THE GOSPEL

AND THE LAWS OF Florida AT Ormond Beach, Fla

THIS 29th DAY OF May IN THE YEAR OF OUR LORD 1962

WITNESSES:

James H. Clark

Ernest E Haddad
MINISTER

71

Doug, Doug's Dad, Craig, Cory, Calvin - 1962

Wedding Day - 1962

Doug & Lois
with family 1963

Doug & Lois 1967

Doug going to work
1963

Doug & Cory - 1962

Chuck, Calvin, Doug, Cory, Craig - 1962

Calvin, Doug, & Cory - 1962

74

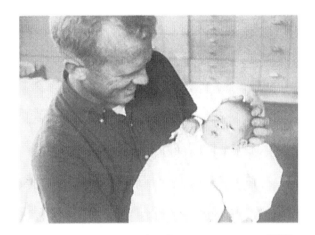

Doug and Andy 1964

Andy and Mom
Daytona Beach 1966

Andy and Doug
1966

Mom, Andy and brothers 1966
(before seatbelts)

Daytona Beach • 1966

Craig, Lois, Chuck and Andy

Conrad & Doug in Atlanta - 1966

Bahamas - 1966

Doug & George Baker

Ginny, George Baker, and Lois

Rose Bay Campground,
Port Orange 1970

Chino,
California
1975

West End, Grand Bahama - 1971

80

Bahamas 1976

1985

Acapulco - January 29, 1975

82

1985

Easter Beach Run 1985

1986

September 18, 2008

December 23, 1985

9
The Wreckage

Molly took me to the hangar to see the plane not too long after I was released from the hospital. I was shocked at how mangled, totaled and crushed the Aero Commander was.

At first sight, the image was surreal. The initial thought that immediately entered my mind was that I was so glad our son Doug decided not to fly with us that morning. The whole back of the plane and the back-seat area, where he would have been sitting, was completely crushed. He would not have survived.

Based on the pictures of the crash and seeing the wreckage firsthand, it was evident that I had pancaked the plane into the grass field just short of the runway, probably due to a rapid engine surge right before contact. The ground was wet from excessive rains in the area just days prior. In fact, less than a week before the crash, Daytona Beach had a record-setting rainfall of over six inches in one day. The saturated ground did nothing to help my landing, causing the landing gear to pierce into the soft ground surface and not allow the plane to roll.

As far as salvaging the plane, not much remained. One engine was irreparable, but the other engine was still in good enough shape to sell. Surprisingly, we were able to sell that one engine fairly easily. The rest of the plane was basically scrap metal though.

As I stood there, staring at the plane, although my memory had gone blank, I started to vaguely recall the incidents leading up to impact.

What happened was I stalled the airplane at a low altitude while trying to make the runway; maybe because I dropped the landing gear too soon or maybe because I just ran out of air. It really didn't matter though. We slammed hard on the grass just east of Runway 25 Right.

The official FAA investigation would conclude the following:

NTSB Identification: ERA09FA303

14 CFR Part 91: General Aviation

Accident occurred Monday, May 25, 2009 in Daytona Beach, FL

Aircraft: AERO COMMANDER 500 S, registration: N73U

Injuries: 1 Fatal, 1 Serious.

On May 25, 2009, at 0846 eastern daylight time, an Aero Commander 500S, N73U, operated by Commonwealth Aviation Corporation, was substantially damaged following a partial loss of engine power and collision with terrain during a forced landing after takeoff from Daytona Beach International Airport (DAB), Daytona Beach, Florida. The certificated private pilot was seriously injured, and the pilot-rated passenger was killed. Visual meteorological conditions prevailed, and no flight plan was filed for the personal flight that departed about 0843 and was conducted under the provisions of 14 Code of Federal Regulations Part 91.

Preliminary information from the FAA revealed that the airplane was cleared for takeoff from runway 7R. About 1 minute after takeoff, the pilot reported "an engine failure" and announced his intention to return for landing on runway 25R. Witnesses in the vicinity of the airport, approximately 1/2 mile off the departure end of the runway, reported the engine noise from the accident airplane was "surging" as the airplane passed overhead, and one witness described a "radical" turn back to the airport.

Two witnesses, at their motorcycle repair shop, stated that only one engine was running. They added that the engine was "revving," and would then "conk out" before revving up again. As the engine surged, the airplane would "shuffle left and right." One witness described the airplane "just hanging there" as it turned back to the airport. The airplane flew west out of view before it crashed on the 1,000-foot grass safety area prior to the approach end of runway 25R.

A preliminary review of radar data revealed that the pilot declared the emergency when the accident airplane was leveling off at about 1,000 feet, about 1.75 miles from the departure end of the runway. During the turn back to the airport, the airplane descended to 700 feet, then climbed back to 1,100 feet. During the descent to the airport, the data showed the airplane at 93 knots, 700 feet and 1 mile from the runway, and 90 knots, at 500 feet and 1/2 mile from the runway.

A review of FAA and pilot records revealed that the pilot held a private pilot certificate, with ratings for airplane single-engine land, airplane single-engine sea, airplane multiengine land, and instrument airplane. His most recent FAA third-class medical certificate was issued on July 17, 2007. The pilot reported 1,250 total hours of flight experience on that date. Review of the pilot's logbook revealed approximately 1,470 total hours of flight experience; of which, 570 hours of which were in the same make and model as the accident airplane.

The airplane was examined at the site on May 25, 2009. There was no odor of fuel, and all major components were accounted for at the scene. The airplane came to rest on flat, grassy terrain on the airport property, 267 feet prior to the approach end of runway 7R. The wreckage path was oriented 240 degrees magnetic and was 140 feet in length. The airplane came to rest oriented 360 degrees.

The wreckage was removed from the site and the examination was resumed on the parking ramp on May

26, 2007. Examination of the cockpit revealed that the left and right fuel valve switches and the left and right fuel boost switches were in the "on" position.

The fuel system had a capacity of 226 gallons, was serviced through a single port on top of the left wing, and the tanks were interconnected to a center fuel sump that fed both engines. The fuel cells were opened through access panels and each were intact and contained only trace amounts of fuel. The airplane was leveled, the drain petcock was opened at the center fuel cell sump, and 1 quart of fuel was drained. The sample appeared clean and contained trace amounts of sediment and water.

Sometime after the investigation was complete, I received a tip about someone stealing gas out of the Aero Commander while it was in our hangar. This tip came from a very reliable source; someone I trusted. In fact, she witnessed the crime with her own two eyes. It was a complicated situation because we were letting someone else share the hangar space and sometimes lease the LearJet from us. Apparently, he didn't have enough money to put fuel into the LearJet for a charter he had booked, so he "borrowed it" from the Aero Commander. There were actually a couple of people (one was a known felon with a long rap sheet, we would later discover) who had access to our airplane hangar.

I chose not to pursue going after the guy that stole the gas out of our plane. As a pilot, I should not have flown the plane with an inoperative fuel gauge anyway, even for maintenance purposes. Plus, there was no benefit in pursuing that fight. It wasn't going to bring my father back to life; rather, just cause me to have to rehash the accident and spend a lot of time trying to resolve something on principle that really would bring no resolution to me. I wrote it off as an unforeseen event that was out of my control, much like the crash of the economy. You just have to maneuver around things like that when they happen and move on with life.

Focus on the important things. Live each day to its fullest, because it may be your last day. Live in the moment now and try to always remember that life can change in an instant. All you can do is control how you react.

I always try to use my gut instinct and my gut instinct told me to put the cause of the lack of fuel in the plane behind me as quickly as I could. My father taught me to follow my gut. His teachings came in very handy in making my decision in regard to this dilemma and pursuing legal retribution. I did, however, learn the importance of checking people's credentials and background history. I also have made carefully checking the fuel levels in my airplane before every flight the most important preflight check!

Mistakes fail in their mission of helping the person who blames them on the other fellow.
~ Henry Haskins

10
Thank You, Luck

Would you rather be lucky or talented? It's a philosophical question worth pondering. I've known a lot of talented people who suffered bad luck and struggled in life. I also know others who always seem lucky. I remind myself each day how lucky I am. In fact, every morning, as soon as I wake up, I spend about 10 minutes sitting in a chair meditating to "program" my mind for the day. One of my primary mantras is gratitude and staying in the present moment. I "write it on my heart that today will be the best day of my life."

I believe in then expressing this gratitude; sending thank you cards and making check-in calls. In the spirit of my belief, Molly and I took some fresh-baked, homemade cookies to the Daytona Beach Airport fire station one day not too long after I got out of the hospital. With a smile on my face and appreciation in my heart, I presented those cookies to the firefighters and first responders who saved my life.

Volusia Fire Services Lt. Michael Hackathorn, Volusia County firefighter Glenn Ingermann, and Daytona Beach Fire Lt. Michael Harvey were of those in attendance. They, along with their colleagues, were quite taken aback with our presence and gesture. "We rarely get a thank you, let alone in person," more than one of them expressed.

The firefighters would describe to me, in detail, the scene when they arrived at the crash and how they removed the windshield so they could get access to put a backboard on me. Then they told me how they lifted me from the cockpit. I vaguely remember being lifted from the plane as I drifted in and out of consciousness. It was an interesting conversation about the details of the rescue. It was like piecing together a dream on the way to work the next day.

My head had smashed into the airplane's dashboard upon impact. When it hit, a gauge crushed my lower right eye socket, only about an inch below my eye. An inch made the difference between losing that eye and keeping it.

"If that gauge had hit you an inch higher, you'd be wearing a patch on your eye right now," one of the firemen said, shaking his head in disbelief of the fact that I walked through the door and was sitting across from him, looking at him with two good eyes.

The dashboard peeled the skin on my forehead back, essentially scalping me.

"And if your scalp had peeled back any further, or if the cut had gone any deeper, you probably would have bled out before we got to you," another hero added.

I also punctured my lung and tore my aorta; however, the worst injury would end up being my back. I crushed two vertebrae in my lower spine.

"If we had to extract you any quicker, say in the case of fire, your spinal cord would have been in much more jeopardy of being severed. This would have killed you instantly, or certainly paralyzed you."

I was in and out of consciousness. Fortunately, the plane had not caught fire, but I do remember being hot and complaining to the firefighters angrily about the heat. One of the firefighters present was the same guy I had been cursing at to get me out of the plane. I remember how weird but reassuring his fire-resistant gloved hand felt. I remember thinking, as the blood from my forehead dripped onto his glove, "this is bad," and I lost consciousness again. He smiled at me with compassion and, when he finished chewing his cookie, he said, "I was scared for you, buddy. It was not a pleasant sight. Your father was DOA, and you were rough, real rough. Happy to see you here though. It means a lot."

Sometimes luck comes in the form of irony. This would be the case in regard to the cause of the crash. "Lack of fuel in the plane probably saved your life though. I think it prevented the plane from exploding and burning."

I chuckled because I remembered, and they confirmed, that I was complaining about the heat. The heat seemed to compound my discomfort tremendously. It was late May and it was a hot and humid Florida day. The sun was beating down on me. I wanted to be out of the confines of the crumpled airplane to get some relief from the heat in the cramped metal space.

My next memory was being thankful for the air conditioning in the ambulance, thus ending my impatient struggle with the prior oppressive heat. Impressive was that I had the cognitive ability to appreciate the temperature change and understand that I was in air conditioning. I could have suffered much more traumatic head injuries that would have affected my brain, my senses, and my memory. Again, I would call that luck.

Fortunately, for me, it was a short ambulance ride from the airport to Halifax Hospital. Had I crashed farther away, in the woods or somewhere difficult to access, I would have certainly not survived. "Thank God you crashed at the airport so we could get to you quickly, plus Halifax Hospital was a short drive away. You're a lucky guy, man."

Someone, I believe maybe the Lt. said, with a great degree of certainty, "If any of those factors had been different, you probably wouldn't be standing here today."

By taking the time to express gratitude and fellowship with these heroes, I was able to express my newfound respect for first responders and medical staff. They saved my life and I am forever grateful.

I wrapped up the visit with a round of heart-felt hugs for everyone. Hugging had become a new trend for me, and I wasn't ashamed to admit it. Express your feelings. Thank those who are deserving. Expect nothing in life but appreciate everything that comes your way, especially good luck.

Andy and Molly thanking his rescuers.
Photo by Daytona Beach News Journal

11
Freedom to Go for Broke

When I came home from the hospital, I had to face the fact that my father was gone, and the success of All Aboard Properties was all on me now. And it happened at the worst possible time, in regard to the economy, since the Great Depression.

Thanks to the hard work of the All Aboard team (who all agreed to take a 10% cut in wages to help us cut our company expenses during the Recession), the business was still alive – and, thankfully, so was I.

It took me about 3 months after the accident to start driving again and return to the office. Emma, who was 15 years old at the time and had a restricted driver's license, was sometimes my chauffeur; driving me to Rotary meetings, etc. when Molly was picking up Camille or Doug.

I had a miraculous recovery, considering what I had been through and the condition I was in just a short time prior. It was awesome to pull through it all and finally get back to work. But with medical bills piling up and the recession bearing down on us, it only took a few months to exhaust the cash reserves (CDs and such) that had been set aside to float the business and pay my family's living expenses.

When our CFO, Mike Polito, analyzed our financial situation, he immediately said, "Operations should support itself." However, the operations department wasn't supporting itself due to the massive debt we had incurred over the years to fuel our company's growth. We all just kept thinking that the recession would end at any time, but it kept dragging on and on. Our average self-storage occupancy dipped to an all-time low of 55%, which allowed us to pay all our operating expenses and interest on our business loans, but not the principal payments. Tenants were walking away from their "extra stuff," leaving us with sudden, unexpected vacancies.

In the past, my father and I were able to rapidly grow the company by leveraging assets, which was fine during times of growth in bull markets, but during recessions, you're left with a lot of heavy baggage in the form of debt. We learned some very important lessons about debt during those times. Today, we have restructured our debt and we can dip down to a 45% occupancy rate and still cash flow. We've stress-tested our break-even analysis because we learned to have cash reserves, run a more lean operation, and to be conservative and not go into too much debt. Learning these lessons came the hard way and required a new mindset and attitude. The survival of the company would depend on me dealing with lenders in ways that I never had the need or gumption to do in the past.

When Grampa Doug died, the company had $93 million in debt. Doug was a risk-taker. He borrowed, leveraged, and developed. We moved money from pocket to pocket or property to property to float projects. Before the accident, we had already started the process of renegotiating with lenders because we realized that, if the economy didn't improve, we were on a sinking ship. We thought we were doing the right thing by proactively going to the banks to renegotiate our debt before things got really bad and we defaulted. Ironically, the banks (and our attorneys) told us that we had to go into default before we could renegotiate the loans with a special loan servicer. So, we tried that.

Intentionally defaulting was very difficult for us because it went against our morals. We had always paid our loans like clockwork, so it was tough to take this approach. We kept current on the properties that weren't upside down, but we tried not making payments on problematic loans that were with big, national banks. Then they would send a default/foreclosure notice and we would get scared, give in and pay. We didn't have the fortitude and gumption to follow through on the defaults. That was before my accident.

After the economy tanked, some of my former loan officers became "workout specialists" during the recession. So, after the accident, I hired one of them to help me negotiate with my lenders.

We came up with a whole bankruptcy plan, but luckily, I never actually had to file bankruptcy. I just used the tactic to show the lenders that was an option. It was a bizarre and uncomfortable poker game. On multiple occasions, process servers came to our house at 6am to deliver court papers to me.

The plane crash helped me deal with this situation in several weird ways. The first being the story itself. Being in a plane crash was a heck of an excuse and a powerful story to tell the lenders. "My father died, I almost died, I can't pay the note..." Secondly, I had a different state of mind after the accident. I wasn't ruffled as much, despite the extreme financial stress. My priorities became, "Am I alive? Can I walk? Can I get dressed?" I became braver because I didn't care about certain things as much. I now had more gumption and courage to tell the truth: "We can't pay you." Previously, both my father and I knew that's what we needed to do, but it was just very hard to actually do it.

After the accident, I tried to adopt the "jingle mail" attitude (with loans that I did not personally guarantee) that many other developers and property owners had already employed. Jingle mail is when you mail the keys back to the lender and say, "Here you go... here's your upside-down property." My "workout guy" was like that. He was a tough talker.

In 2015, I gave the Clark Office Building to the bank so they could sell it at auction. The numbers on the property were crazy. It cost us $7 million to build in 2001. After it was built, we leased it all out. The tenants were paying $25/square foot which made the building worth around $7 million at that time. We borrowed $5 million on the building. We had a partial construction loan of $3 million that we paid off and then used the remaining money to develop other new projects.

In 2006, we could have sold the entire building to the tenant on the 3rd floor for $10 million, but we didn't since we were so set on the "buy and hold" real estate philosophy. We had 5-year leases that matured in 2007 and 2009. In 2009, everyone moved out. All the tenants felt the crunch of the economy and folded. Even Halifax Hospital moved out of the building's entire first floor.

So, in 2009, with all the vacancy, the building was only worth $3 million, and I still owed almost $5 million. The big, national lender who held the note on the property was super stubborn. Even after I had rectified almost all of the other debts, this lender wouldn't budge, so I gave them the keys in

2015 after 5 years of negotiations but was able to buy the building back at auction for about $2 million.

We had to restructure other projects as well, like the Portofino Townhomes on Riverside Drive by our office. We thought those town homes would sell for $1 million each. We had hard costs of $500k each, not counting the land. In 2010 and 2011, we partnered with the lender (Floridian Bank), marketed the town homes and sold the two riverfront units for about $400,000 and the other 6 units sold for about $300,000. Floridian Bank and I both took the hit together. We endured some tough times together.

It took a long time for the economy to come back and no one knew when it would happen. For the most part, everyone was going through the same thing and they understood. It was scary and rough, but, like the plane crash, I survived.

12
First Flight

I surf when I can and I live just north of New Smyrna Beach, Florida; the "shark bite capital of the world." I personally know people who have been nipped by sharks and I've heard stories of surfers, like Bethany Hamilton, who lost an arm to a shark attack while surfing and then rebounded back to greatness in the sport. I often wondered if I could get back on a surfboard if that happened to me. Well, if I draw a parallel to flying, then the answer is yes.

Even after my horrific accident and the loss of my father, I still had the desire to fly. Just a short three weeks after the crash, while I was still in recovery, my Mom told me she thought I should fly again. In fact, she encouraged me to go for it.

In December 2009, just seven months after the accident, I decided to take the family to the Bahamas for Christmas break on a commercial flight from Orlando to Nassau. Although I would not be the pilot, it would be my first time back in the air since the crash. The flight was a bit spooky and a little uncomfortable mostly because my back was still healing.

In a coincidental turn of events, my son Doug got sick with what we thought was a stomach bug right before we were supposed to leave on this trip. Molly decided she better stay home with him and I should take the two girls to Bahamas anyway while she stayed with Doug. The scenario ended up somewhat reminiscent of Doug missing the flight seven months earlier that surely would have cost him his life.

While I was in the Bahamas with Emma and Camille, Doug's condition worsened and Molly took him to Dr. Chopra, our pediatrician. Dr. Chopra checked Doug's blood sugar. It was over 700 mg/dl. Coma and death can occur when blood sugar levels get that high. She told Molly to take Doug to Halifax Hospital immediately.

At Halifax, they stabilized Doug and he was taken by ambulance to Arnold Palmer Children's Hospital in Orlando where he was diagnosed with type-1 Diabetes, a lifelong condition in which his pancreas produces no insulin.

Emma, Camille and I flew back to Orlando from Nassau as Doug was to be discharged from Arnold Palmer. We learned about carb counting and giving Doug his insulin injections. He now uses an insulin pump.

Sometime in 2010, I remember watching a video simulation of Captain Sully landing in the Hudson river. The intensity of the simulation made my palms sweaty. It was a very similar situation to what I endured in that he lost both engines at takeoff. Sully had to make a split-second decision as to what to do and where to land. There were many more lives (155 to be exact) at stake on US Airways Flight 1549. Miraculously, Captain Sully safely landed the Airbus jet on the Hudson River without losing a single life. Wow, I thought; what an amazing feat. This miracle empowered me to get back in the cockpit.

In July 2011, I met with the Federal Aviation Association (FAA) examiner about how I could reinstate my pilot's license so I could fly again. I couldn't get my license back until I passed instrument check ride tests with an FAA examiner in a twin-engine piston aircraft (the same type of aircraft I crashed). I started instrument flight training in a Beechcraft Duchess (a four-place twin engine training aircraft) owned by Air America, a flight school who happened to be a tenant of mine at our hangar complex.

I went through three months of re-training and rigorous check rides with an FAA instructor. In one particular check ride, the instructor told me I was "too lackadaisical." His comment humbled me. Had I not been through the accident, I might not have been as receptive to his feedback and commentary. Nonetheless, it was good training and I learned a lot. My pilot's license was reinstated in January 2012.

I bought an older model V-tail Beechcraft Bonanza in November 2012, which I then traded in for a 2015 glass-cockpit Bonanza in May 2016. In April 2019, I traded in the Bonanza for a new 2018 twin piston Beechcraft Baron. I also bought a new Sports Cruiser light sport plane in 2017 for my son Doug to fly and get his pilot's license.

The process of going through the training and recertification taught me that there is always room for improvement and that we should never stop learning and practice, practice, practice. I now apply this mindset to all areas of my life--both personally and professionally.

Andy with his Bonanza in Miami 2017

13
Port Orange

I still think about my father almost every day. I can't help but continue to ask him for business advice out of habit even though he's gone. He's my guardian angel and part of my "team of light from the other side," guiding me through my life and helping me with business decisions.

His picture hangs on the Wall of Fame in the Port Orange City Hall, so I see it when I go there on business. On July 4th, 2009, just five weeks after the crash, the city had an induction ceremony for him after our All Aboard employees nominated him to be in the Port Orange Hall of Fame. I spoke at the ceremony in spite of my rough condition at the time. I pledged to have our company continue the good work that my father started in Port Orange.

Here is a timeline of our business activities in the City of Port Orange:

1962: Doug designed and built houses off U.S 1 on Fox Place, Lafayette Street, and Orange Avenue, just south of Dunlawton Avenue. Some were spec homes (built on "speculation" -- without having a specific buyer). These homes would usually sell before they were completed. He would also build some custom homes in that part of Port Orange near the city's only little league baseball field.

1963: Doug and two other young builders: Bob Powell and Bob Mohr formed MPC Builders. The trio was introduced by Ralph Frederick, another builder from Ormond Beach. MPC started buying land in small phases from Marcel Marone, a Montreal, Canada investor who purchased 450 acres of undeveloped land in Port Orange in 1956 and then MPC started developing Commonwealth Estates off Commonwealth Blvd., which is a subdivision for manufactured homes. MPC developed these lots themselves by hand-digging a sewer line from US1 to serve the subdivision and forming and pouring the sidewalks themselves.

1965: MPC sold all the homes for the subdivision from a sales lot on US1 and then set up homes themselves. This sales division was called Commonwealth Mobile Homes Sales, Inc. which would continue over the next 15 years to sell and set up over 2,000 manufactured homes all in Port Orange owned and developed by Doug and his partners. (Doug later renamed this corporation Commonwealth Aviation Corp. to operate the hangar leasehold at the Daytona Beach International Airport.) During this time in the 1970's, the population of Port Orange boomed from about 400 registered voters in the early 1960's to about 12,000 in the late 1970's.

1968: MPC started Briarwood Estates, their first lot-rental community for manufactured homes where homeowners pay lot rent. They sold Briarwood in 1973.

1969: Our family moved from 1225 Thompson Place in Daytona Beach to a large historic home at 5120 Riverside Drive in Allandale (annexed into Port Orange in the 1980's). We also owned a small 19-unit trailer park behind our house on US1 called Sunny Skies, which is where the Clark Office Building is today.

1970: MPC built Commonwealth Plaza on Nova Road and started Rose Bay Campground. They also owned an LP gas company to sell gas for cooking and heating to the residents in their communities. I used to read the gas meters each month at the resident's homes when I was 15 years old. My brothers Chuck and Calvin did that job before me. Also, during this time, Doug and Bob started Pathfinders campground directory which operated out of Commonwealth Plaza.

1973-1981: Tanglewood Estates manufactured home community north of Commonwealth Blvd. was developed.

1974-1980: Maplewood Estates manufactured home community near the corner of Nova Road and Spruce Creek Road was developed.

1977-1982: Laurelwood Estates manufactured home subdivision off Madeline Ave. was developed.

1978: Doug and Bob Powell attended their first Self-Service Storage Association (now called the Self Storage Association) convention to learn about the self storage business. They were planning their first self storage facility on Nova Road after Bob Powell had seen other "mini warehouse" facilities being built. (Bob Mohr had left MPC Builders in the early 1970's.)

1979: Doug and Bob Powell bought about 160 acres south of Taylor Road across from Spruce Creek High School about developed one-acre lot subdivisions for customers to build their own homes in Spruce Creek Woods Estates, Hensel Hill East & West and Pheasant Run East & West.

1983: Maplewood Self Storage (now called Port Orange Depot) opened. We built this property ourselves. We had a small crew of my brothers Chuck and Craig and two other brothers: Bradley and Kendall Rauch as well as our supervisor, Bill West. I helped with the construction labor after school and during the summers when I wasn't mowing the grass or cleaning the pool at one of our manufactured home communities. We were the same crew that had set up all the manufactured homes in Maplewood, Tanglewood and Laurelwood Estates. At Maplewood Self Storage, we formed and poured all the concrete slabs. We subcontracted the masonry blockwork, but we installed the entire roof and all the rollup doors. We also built the rental office for the facility and installed the landscaping. Craig and his wife, Cheryl, were the first managers of this self storage facility. They lived on site in the resident managers apartment behind the office.

1984: We built Regency Office Center in our old work yard next to our main office at 5652 Isabelle Ave. to fulfill the demand of customers at Maplewood Self Storage wanting to have an office with their storage unit. Also, at this time, we built South Daytona Storage & Offices in South Daytona. In 1988, Doug and I bought and later doubled the size of both Daytona Self Storage and The Storage Box (now Jimmy Ann Depot) in Daytona Beach. Doug and Bob Powell had split up their partnership by this time.

1990: We bought a former Lowes Lumber building on Nova Road and converted it into our Nova Depot self storage which we called Stowaway Storage at the time. We also purchased Florida Records document storage & retrieval in Port Orange and relocated it to Nova Depot.

1994-2002: I found out through Debbie Connors, the President of the Port Orange/South Daytona Chamber of Commerce, that the Grace Episcopal Church of Port Orange was looking for a new home for its historic parish hall. So, Doug and I arranged to have it transported one mile south along Ridgewood Ave. to Doug's backyard. Chuck and Craig helped renovate the parish hall to become the Chapel in the Garden wedding venue. Doug then bought the Pink House Antique Store on Ridgewood Ave. and renovated it to become the Tavern in the Garden for wedding receptions. The neighboring Allandale Apartments was also purchased on Riverside Drive; its historic heart pine lumber was salvaged for reuse on the property for expanding other buildings, and then the shell of the building was demolished. With the addition and careful renovation of a train car, Agatha's cottage, and the Snow White Cottage, the area is now called the Estate on the Halifax.

1998: We built our Westport Depot in phases off Williamson Blvd. and we bought and renovated Masonova Plaza in Daytona Beach.

2001: We built the Clark Office Building. We also purchased and renovated the Halifax Shopping Center in Holly Hill, which we sold in 2004 and replaced it with the Sunshine Park Mall in South Daytona.

2004: We purchased Treasure Isle Estates manufactured home community next to Maplewood Estates.

2005: We purchased the Port Orange Flea Market on Ridgewood Ave. (now All Aboard Flea & Farmers Market).

2006: We purchased the Chick Fil A ground lease on Dunlawton Ave.

2007: We built the Portofino Townhomes on Riverside Drive and my brother Craig was the construction supervisor. Also, in 2007, we bought a portfolio of four more self storage facilities in South Daytona and Ormond Beach.

Today, in Port Orange, we still own four self storage facilities, Maplewood & Treasure Isle Estates, the Clark Office Building, the All Aboard Flea & Farmers Market, Regency Office Center and my family owns and operates the Estate on the Halifax wedding venue. We are also now getting permits for our 17th self storage location on Taylor Road by Spruce Creek Fly-Inn.

Andy and Mom 1964

Grampa Eharoshe, Andy,
Cory and Sam Karr 1964

Andy and Calvin 1964

Cory, Andy and Calvin 1965

Front steps of 1225 Thompson
Place, Daytona Beach where we
lived from 1963-1969
Calvin, Chuck, Andy, Cory & Craig

1964

Andy 1966

Andy and Calvin
1967

Cory, Craig, Chuck and Andy 1967

1968

1968

5120 Riverside Dr., Allandale
(now part of Port Orange) FL

Andy, Calvin and Cory

Andy, Calvin and Chuck
1973

Andy and Doug 2005

1974

14
The All Aboard Brand

Even though my Father and I loved airplanes, the logo of the family business is a train. There's a story behind that...

My father and I used to analyze other businesses to get ideas on ways to improve our own business. We found role models in other local family businesses like Thompson Pump, Conrad Yelvington Distributors and the Root Company.

The Root Company displayed Susie Root's Teddy bear collection at the Museum of Arts and Sciences in the 1990's. The Root Company needed to temporarily move the bears and the large display while the museum did some renovations, so we rented them a storage space in one of our T-hangars.

My father had worked at a rail yard in Chicago when he was on summer vacation from high school, and he had a fondness for 1940's passenger trains. Coincidentally, the Root family owned some train cars which they stored at their headquarters on Fentress Blvd. in Daytona Beach. We discussed trading storage space with them for their dining train car, but Doug located a bar-car for sale on a property up in Iowa. He bought it and had it trucked down here and put on the property at The Estate. He and James "Bo" Alvis carefully renovated the train car to be as authentic as possible.

When I started searching for a name for our growing brand of self storage, I wanted something that was meaningful and valuable. When I first started working at the company, it was called MPC Builders.

At first, each self storage complex had a different name that was based on their location. Maplewood Self Storage was next to Maplewood Mobile Home Park, South Daytona Storage was (of course) in South Daytona, and Airport storage was at the airport. Those were the three self storage facilities we had back in 1986 when I graduated from the University of Florida with a bachelor's degree in Public Relations with a minor in business.

I started as the general manager of MPC Builders in 1986 and my job was to run these three self storage facilities and the sales team associated with them. We were really just a small construction company that was growing into a retail self storage operator.

In 1988 when my father and Bob Powell split up, it was just Doug and I left to grow the business. So, we started buying up more storage facilities. Since it was just us, I changed the name of our company to from MPC Builders to "Clark Properties" because that's what people would say: "Oh, it's another Clark property." We kept that name for almost 20 years.

I came up with the name "All Aboard Storage" in 2001. There was another storage company named All Aboard MIni-Storage based in California. An ex-football player owned it. He was buying property from the railroad land and developing storage facilities on that land. I thought it was a clever idea and a catchy name. Imitation is the highest form of flattery, right?

I also liked "All Aboard" because it started with the letter 'A' and would be the first self storage listing in the phone book - and, back then, the phone book was our main sources of advertisement and marketing.

The name change created some confusion for employees. Some people would say that they worked for Clark Properties, while others would say they worked for All Aboard Storage. And so, in 2014, we did a branding initiative to decide whether we should be All Aboard Properties and All Aboard Storage or Clark Properties and Clark Storage since I wanted one logo and one brand name. We voted amongst ourselves and on Facebook. We discovered from a customer focus group that we had the image and persona of a fun company that took cruises together as a celebration for attaining our annual budget goals. We changed all branding to reflect All Aboard at that time.

Our new name and brand was apropos because it could apply to a plane, a train or a cruise ship; but really it means, "come all aboard and rent from us."

The original All Aboard Storage logo from the early 2000's was a train conductor with a megaphone yelling "All Aboard!"

We've grown a lot as a result of our branding. In fact, we now have a management company that manages other companies' self-storage facilities. My daughter, Emma, and Mike Polito handle this most of this third-party management. The properties we currently manage are in The Villages in the Orlando area.

Grampa Doug's dad (my grandfather) operated his own bakeries in northern Illinois, opening them from town to town. And his father (my great grandfather) had his own farm and did construction in northern Illinois. Grampa Doug initially learned how to do carpentry work from his grandfather.

I think it's amazing that the entrepreneurial spirit permeated my family for generations. Entrepreneurship is definitely ingrained in the Clark family brand.

The All Aboard Properties company slogan is "Always on Track." This slogan not only ties into the train logo and theme, but it acts as a reminder for us to always remain focused on our goals.

Former logos (2003-2013)   Current Logos (since 2013)

Sunshine Park Mall, South Daytona, 2004

1988 Yellow Pages Ad

1993 Yellow Pages Ad

1994 Yellow Pages Ad

134

2007 Yellow Pages Ad

135

2008 News Journal Ad

15
Family Dynamics

Family is very important to me, and I'm blessed to be a part of a family that has all worked together in some aspect of the family business. I have four half-brothers who all carry the Gittner last name from my mom's previous marriage: Chuck, Craig, Cory and Calvin. My father had two sons (Greg and David Clark) from his first marriage. I'm the youngest of all the boys. Timing has been a major factor in bringing the family together in business and also taking some of us off on our own individual pursuits.

Chuck and Craig worked for my father during the 1970's and 1980's helping build the manufactured home communities and our first self-storage facilities. Chuck and Craig then formed Gittner Construction and built custom homes in Port Orange during the 1990's and 2000's. Chuck now builds displays for Stihl tools at different stores and venues around the southeast U.S. Craig now runs the Estate on the Halifax, our Port Orange wedding business that is still family-owned, by Craig, me, my mom, brothers Cory and Calvin, and Craig's daughter, Cara.

Greg and David Clark grew up at the Argosy Motel with their mom (Grampa Doug's first wife), Phyllis. David passed away in 1980 and Greg and his family went on to operate the Argosy after Phyllis also passed away. Greg later sold the Argosy property to Volusia County for beachfront parking.

Cory has lived in Miami since 1980 and has his own advertising and public relations agency there called Meditech. In high school when Cory wasn't a lifeguard with the Volusia County Beach Patrol, he painted and installed mailboxes for new residents of the manufactured home communities.

Calvin, who also worked for MPC Builders during high school, is now the pastor at the Presbyterian church in Port Orange on Clyde Morris. He officiated Doug's funeral at his church.

I started working for my father when I was 12 years old after school and during the summers in Briarwood Estates (manufactured home community) helping sweep the gutters in the streets. My pay was 60 cents per hour. I continued working at MPC Builders throughout my teen years at the manufactured home communities and when we built our first self-storage facility. I mostly laid sod, did lawn care, swimming pool maintenance and construction labor.

When I graduated college and I had the desire to join the family business, and the business had an immediate need for a manager to oversee the two existing self-storage facilities and their four employees as well as the third facility that was under construction and about to come onboard - the addition of which would also necessitate hiring another two employees to manage. My father and his partner were busy managing other development projects and needed someone to handle this part of the business. I had the desire to do the job and my father and his partner had the trust in me to give me the chance. I was given the opportunity to learn and take on additional responsibilities. Good timing steered me into what has become a lifelong career.

Oftentimes, family businesses can fail or stagnate when the patriarch isn't willing to delegate or give up responsibility or control. In other cases, the next generation might not be willing or capable of taking on the responsibility of the business. Fortunately, the next generation of Clarks is now active in the family business. My daughter, Emma, has become an integral part of All Aboard Properties as the HR Coordinator. Her active involvement and participation in the business helps ensure that the Clark family legacy in All Aboard Properties will continue, and I'm grateful for that.

Although the entire family may not work together directly at this time, we are always there for each other in some capacity. A great example is how my family was instrumental in helping me recover from the crash, both mentally and physically. My brothers visited me at home during my recovery on many occasions.

On one visit, Calvin told me the story of how he found out about the crash and Grampa Doug's passing from my daughter, Emma, while he and the rest of his family were driving to the beach for Memorial Day. He diverted course and went straight to Mom's house to notify her. Mom recalled how Calvin didn't even have to say a word to her when he showed up unexpectedly that morning. His quivering lip told the whole story as he stood at her door speechless and teary-eyed.

I'm so sorry that Mom had to deal with the loss of my father while I was still in the ICU, but she was strong-willed and stayed by my side and with my family quite a bit. While dealing with immense emotional pain of her own, Mom helped me mentally manage my physical pain and wean myself off of the pain pills once I came out of the coma. There truly is no love greater than that of a mother.

Timing is everything when it comes to business. We've all heard the phrase "buy low, sell high" - well, it takes the right timing for that formula to work. When it comes to family, timing is important too. We all have our ebbs and flows in life. Oftentimes, family comes together in times of need or at the holidays. But know this, no matter what situation you're in, and regardless of the timing, always take the time to let your family know you love and appreciate them.

"Success comes when people act together; failure tends to happen alone. You can't make positive choices for the rest of your life without an environment that makes those choices easy, natural, and enjoyable. Always go with your passions. Never ask yourself if it's realistic or not."
~Deepak Chopra

Andy graduating Spruce
Creek High School 1982

My first solo in 1987 with
Daytona Beach Aero Club
Instructor Charley Herm who
also signed off check rides
with Grampa Doug in 1955.

Doug, Mom and Molly
1989 at Molly's house

142

Molly, Andy and Mom 1992

Andy and Molly after getting married April 24, 1993
outside St. Paul's Basilica, Daytona Beach

Doug, Gramma Clark, Molly and Emma 1994

1996

Disney Cruise 2002

Camille, Doug and Emma 2003

November 2009

2020

Andy & Molly's granddaughter Zena
Clark (Camille's daughter) in 2018

Andy & Zena 2019

16
Lessons Learned

The greatest lesson I learned from my plane crash is that life is short and can change in an instant. The financial crash has taught me to never run out of cash, just like with flying, you never want to run out of gas.

There were many parallels between the plane crash and the business crash. Coincidentally, my father had compared the recession to a plane crashing just one year prior to our actual crash--talk about foreshadowing!

There were warning signs associated with both crashes; like the broken fuel gauge and the market reports.

The irony is that if it hadn't been for the plane crash, I might not have survived the economy crash. I probably would have had a heart attack from the stress of the business. The plane crash and ensuing recovery process made me stronger and prepared me to deal with the business in ways that I previously wasn't capable of.

First, the plane crash gave me an attitude of gratitude to be alive. Second, it gave me the gumption to lay it on the line in negotiations with banks and lenders and not hold back. My newfound mentality told me that, 'I survived a plane crash, I can survive this difficult meeting.' I also knew that losing a property, if it happened, would pale in comparison to losing my life, a family member, or the ability to walk, talk or care for myself.

I learned to be more conservative in regard to growing the business. I reduced debt and now strive to keep it low. We run leaner operations and find creative ways to be more efficient and save money whenever and wherever possible. We created cash reserves for rainy days and inevitable economic slowdowns.

Having a capable co-pilot to keep you calm and help you navigate and land the plane in an emergency is a very good thing. My father's last words, "Head for the numbers," still resonates in my mind today. Fortunately, I had a great team of copilots at work to do the same for me while I was in a coma, and then during my recovery.

Life happens and there are certain things we'll never control, but what I learned is that how you react to situations is the most important thing. Controlling your reactions is the true success.

I also add persistence as a key to overcoming adversity.

We're a third-generation family business --
how did we survive the past 70 years? It helps to
realize that, in a family business, you wear different
"hats" -- as a family member and as an employee or
part-owner of a business. You can be a brother and,
at the same time, be a business partner with your
brother, for example.

Your business with your brother might fail,
but he's still your brother. I think family is more
important than the business.

It's also best to have one person at the top of
the business in charge and for everyone to know
and respect each other's roles in the business and in
the family.

Another bit of advice is to have a succession
plan in place for the business. Establish a trust and
make provisions to pay the trustee in the event they
have to step in and run the business in emergency
situations. Define roles and responsibilities for your
heirs. I would also suggest appointing a sole
executor of your estate to make the decision-
making process easier and to cut down on family
disputes.

As technology keeps advancing, I think it is
important to continue learning and networking
through the Chambers of Commerce, service
organizations like Rotary, 1 Million Cups, peer
groups, trade organizations, and at local colleges.
Take time to educate yourself by listening to or
reading good business books.

One of my favorite books is "The Fifth Agreement" by Don Miguel Ruiz. In this book, Mr. Ruiz does a masterful job at identifying and explaining five rules to live by. Not only do I strive to follow these 'agreements' on a personal level, but I have shared them with my professional family at All Aboard Properties and they have become the foundation of our company culture (along with continuous improvement and empowerment). The agreements are:

1. BE IMPECCABLE WITH YOUR WORD. Speak with integrity and say only what you mean.
2. DON'T TAKE ANYTHING PERSONALLY.
3. DON'T MAKE ASSUMPTIONS.
4. ALWAYS DO YOUR BEST.
5. BE SKEPTICAL BUT LEARN TO LISTEN.

Adopting these Agreements has helped me grow and develop, both personally and professionally. It has helped create cohesion and harmony in my family and my business. When your life is in harmony, it's evident in many different ways. I strive to be a good leader and set a positive example for my family and my team of associates. I want to give them the leadership, support and resources to empower them to grow personally and contribute to the company in a meaningful way.

17
Ride the Wave

Surviving the plane crash and the recession taught me to prioritize as well as to control how I react to certain situations ("you can either laugh or cry," my father used to say). I also try to listen to and follow my gut instinct.

One of the most important lessons I've learned in life is that there are going to be inevitable highs and lows. Waves of energy make up matter and permeate time and space; these waves also have peaks and valleys, highs and lows. Once I understood this concept, I have been better able to anticipate and prepare for the low points and, conversely, recognize and appreciate the high points and positives in my life.

About a month before the plane crash, Grampa Doug realized his life was ending and he was itching to check off more items on his life's already very full "bucket list" accomplishments. Even in the face of death, the ultimate adversary, and at what was probably the lowest point of his life, he decided he was going to create one more high point in his life.

He found out he could buy a brand new fully loaded 2008 Chevy Corvette with no money down at the New Smyrna Chevrolet dealership that used to be on US1. I later realized that the dealership just adds the financing costs to the purchase price of the car. So, at the time, you could buy the car for $57,000 cash or $69,000 with zero money down fully financed option. We didn't have any cash left at this point in the recession, so paying cash was not an option. Grampa Doug didn't care about the financing costs.

But Grampa Doug craved some of the material spoils of his hard work that he had rewarded himself with in the past. In the 1950's he had owned a 1955 Corvette convertible that he used to carry around his carpentry tools in its trunk as he would go to work on houses he was building on the North Peninsula of Ormond Beach. In the 1970's, Grampa Doug also bought a new 1976 Corvette for my Mom.

In 2008, he had just sold a 1966 white Corvette that had a manual transmission and no power steering and was too hard for him to steer in his weakened state from his illness.

Grampa Doug loved the power and style of Corvettes. My son now says that only older (middle-aged) guys drive Corvettes, which now makes those once-cool cars passé to the younger generation.

As I drove Grampa Doug down US1 to the Chevrolet dealership in New Smyrna, I told him that, just as he was completing his Bucket List by buying this 2008 Corvette, I had a Bucket List item of my own to tell him.

"I want you to know that I love you," I said. This is something I had never before said to him, but it was something I wanted him to know and I'm glad I took the time to gather the courage to tell him.

"You did a great speech at the Chamber event (The "Tasteful Affair," which we used to host at the Tavern in the Garden)," Grampa Doug replied, which was his way of telling me he was proud of me, and I knew he loved me too. That was a moment and a conversation that I will never forget.

Seven years later, in 2016, inspired by my father and empowered by my own survival and physical and financial recovery, I decided to create more special moments in my life.

One such special moment occurred on the first surf trip I took with my son, Doug, when he was 15 and we went to Nicaragua for a few days by ourselves. We stayed at a small surf resort in the mountains near Popoyo. The resort arranged for us to have a surf guide, Allessio, to drive us the 15 minutes from the resort to Popoyo's main break and surf with us. This main break is an A-frame with left and right walls breaking over a rock shelf. Popoyo can get huge with an outer reef that has a Pipeline-style slab. It is a consistent break at all tides with 300 days a year of offshore winds thanks to a large inland lake.

We had decided on our last night to surf dawn patrol the next morning at Popoyo since we had a few hours before our flight back home.

The waves didn't look that big when we drove up to the car park at Popoyo at first light that last morning. But the car park is about 40' above the beach and, from that vantage point, the wave size can be deceiving. We walked down the steps of that cliff and Allessio did some pre-surfing warm up calisthenics, hopping sideways on the beach, that Doug and I thought was pretty funny.

We were the only ones there since it was so early. We paddled out and the waves were well overhead. The offshore breeze would keep pushing us out to sea, so we were continually paddling around to be in the right spot to catch waves.

I caught a wave or two and then got hammered by an 8' wall of white water as I was paddling back out. My surfboard is a little too big to duck dive so I took a deep breath and pushed the board aside as I dove under the wave. I tumbled under the water for what seemed like a long time, trying not to hit my board, and then I swam and swam to reach the surface, possibly a little too early after the wave passed.

It's easy to hold your breath for 10 or 15 seconds -- except when your heart rate shoots up in a panic.

When I finally reached the surface, I gasped for air and got back on my board. Doug had caught one of the waves in that set and he called out to me, asking if I was okay. I said I was, just in time to look out and see another set wave breaking in front of me. I thought after this wave, I'm heading in. An 8' tall wall of whitewater coming at you as you are paddling toward it really looks huge since your view is from your belly on a surfboard.

I turned around and managed to catch a pretty good final wave back to shore but when I got there, I was actually shaking uncontrollably from the panic of being held underwater.

I sat down on the beach, thankful to be alive, and scanned the waves to see what Doug was up to.

I saw him out there with Allessio catching some waves that were too big for me.

I sat there on the beach happy that our trip had gone so well and that today I would be bringing Doug home safe to Molly. Doug had been my responsibility for the past few days and it had all gone well.

I realized at that moment that not only was he safe, but Doug excelled at surfing and had surpassed me in both courage and skill in regard to surfing. I had taught him everything my brother Craig and others had taught me about surfing, but he had grown and developed on his own, and now he had taken his love of the sport to a much higher level.

Then I reflected on other things that I had taught him or that we had done together after my plane crash - like racquetball at the Port Orange YMCA, snow skiing, snowboarding, wakeboarding, skateboarding and learning to sail a sunfish at the Halifax Sailing Association in Daytona Beach. I then realized that he had surpassed me in those sports as well. He would later get his private pilot's license when he was 18 and become better at "stick and rudder" maneuvers than me.

It was a real tearful ah-ha moment for me as I sat on the beach waiting for Doug to come in from the surf. I was so glad we had the chance to do these things together. I was so proud of the man he was becoming. I also realized that the ultimate accomplishment of a son is to surpass the abilities of his father.

I think all parents want their children to have better lives than they did. This is similar to our core value at All Aboard Properties of Kaizen, or continuous improvement, where every day we try to do better each year compared to the year before.

Just as Grandpa Doug passed the torch to me and I was now continuing the Clark family legacy, it gave me great peace of mind to know that Molly and I have three wonderful children and a granddaughter who are all capable of doing the same.

When you have that peace in your mind, strength in your body, and love in your heart, it's easy to take risks, push the envelope and live life to its fullest.

Waves at Popoya in Nicaragua

Andy surfing Lohis Left in Hudhuranfushi, Maldives 2018

Doug duck diving under a wave in the Maldives 2018

Our surf guide, Allessio, and Doug taking a break
after surfing Popoya in Nicaragua 2016

Doug and Andy in Uluwatu, Bali, Indonesia 2019

Made in the USA
Columbia, SC
02 September 2020

19111934R00093